JÜDISCHES MUSEUM MÜNCHEN
JEWISH MUSEUM MUNICH

Bernhard Purin (Hg. | Ed.)

STADT OHNE JUDEN
CITY WITHOUT JEWS

Die Nachtseite der Münchner Stadtgeschichte
The Dark Side of Munich's History

Edition Minerva   München | Munich 2008

Dieser Katalog erscheint zur gleichnamigen Ausstellung des Jüdischen Museums München vom 24. September 2008 bis 30. August 2009.

This book has been published in conjunction with the exhibition of the same title organized by the Jewish Museum Munich from September 24, 2008 to August 30, 2009.

Die Herstellung des Ausstellungskatalogs wurde durch die freundliche Unterstützung der Peter H. Bach Stiftung ermöglicht.

The publication of the exhibition catalogue was made possible by the generous support of the Peter H. Bach Foundation.

ÜBERSETZUNGEN
\ TRANSLATIONS
Christopher Wynne

LEKTORAT
\ COPYEDITING
Irene Krauss

GRAFIK
\ DESIGN AND LAYOUT
Haller & Haller

GESAMTHERSTELLUNG
\ PRODUCTION
Peschke Druck, München

Die Deutsche Bibliothek verzeichnet diese Publikation in der Deutschen Nationalbibliographie. Detaillierte Angaben sind im Internet über http://dnb.ddb.de abrufbar.

© 2008 Jüdisches Museum München
© 2008 Edition Minerva Hermann Farnung, München

Alle Rechte, auch diejenigen der Übersetzung, der fotomechanischen Wiedergabe und des auszugsweisen Abdrucks, vorbehalten.
All rights reserved.

ISBN 978-3-938832-41-7

Inhalt
Contents

7 Bernhard Purin
Stadt ohne Juden
Die Nachtseite der
Münchner Stadtgeschichte
City without Jews
The Dark Side of
Munich's History

15 Katalog
Catalogue

42 Videotafeln für die Ausstellung
Video Boards for the Exhibition

44 Bibliografie
Bibliography

Martin Kohlbauer
Entwurf für die Ausstellung
*Stadt ohne Juden – Die Nachtseite
der Münchner Stadtgeschichte*
2008

Martin Kohlbauer
Sketch for the exhibition design
*City without Jews—The Dark Side
of Munich's History*
2008

München feiert im Jahr 2008 seinen 850. Geburtstag. Stadtjubiläen werden gerne zum Anlass genommen, mit Stolz auf die Geschichte der Stadt zurückzublicken, sich mit ihr zu identifizieren und das Geschichtsbewusstsein der Stadtgesellschaft zu stärken. Doch wie soll ein Museum auf ein solches Festjahr reagieren, dessen Aufgabe die Vermittlung von Geschichte und Kultur einer Bevölkerungsgruppe ist, die in der 850-jährigen Geschichte der Stadt insgesamt über 400 Jahre von der Teilhabe an eben dieser Stadtgeschichte unfreiwillig und oft auch gewaltsam ausgeschlossen wurde?

STADT OHNE JUDEN

Die Nachtseite der Münchner Stadtgeschichte

von Bernhard Purin

Das Jüdische Museum München spürt in seinem Beitrag zum Stadtgeburtstag genau jenen Jahren in den vergangenen 850 Jahren nach, in denen keine Juden hier leben durften und München eine *Stadt ohne Juden* war. Gleichzeitig werden die Ursachen für Vertreibungen, Verfolgungen und Aufenthaltsverbote aufgezeigt und damit die *Nachtseite der Münchner Stadtgeschichte* thematisiert.

Bereits wenige Jahrzehnte nach der Gründung Münchens im Jahr 1158 finden sich Hinweise auf Juden, die in der Stadt lebten. Mit Abraham „dem Municher" tritt 1229 erstmals ein Münchner Jude – als Zeuge in einem Regensburger Prozess

Throughout 2008 Munich is celebrating its 850th anniversary. Such jubilees are often seen as occasions to look back on a city's history with pride, to identify with it, and to awaken the residents' awareness of its history. But how is a museum—whose task is to promote the history and culture of a certain section of the community—supposed to react to such a festival year, when for more than 400 years in the city's 850-year history, it was involuntarily and often forcefully excluded from taking part?

CITY WITHOUT JEWS

The Dark Side of Munich's History

by Bernhard Purin

In its contribution to the city's anniversary, the Jewish Museum Munich has chosen to trace precisely those times during the last 850 years when Jews were not allowed to live there, when Munich was a *City without Jews*. At the same time, the reasons for their expulsion, persecution, and settlement prohibitions have been highlighted and the issue of the *Dark Side of Munich's History* broached.

References to Jews living in the city can be found in the first few decades after the founding of Munich in 1158. In 1229, the first mention is made of a Munich Jew, Abraham "the Municher," a witness to a court case in Regensburg.

– in Erscheinung. Eine weitere Quelle des 13. Jahrhunderts gibt nicht nur tiefere Einblicke in die erste mittelalterliche Jüdische Gemeinde Münchens, sie ist zugleich Zeugnis ihrer *ersten Katastrophe*, des Pogroms von 1285, bei dem mindestens 68 Juden von Münchner Christen erschlagen oder in ihrer Synagoge verbrannt wurden und deren Namen zum Gedenken im Memorbuch der Jüdischen Gemeinde von Nürnberg aufgeführt sind. Der Vorwurf, einen christlichen Knaben aus rituellen Gründen ermordet zu haben, soll Auslöser für dieses Pogrom gewesen sein. Der gleiche Vorwurf wurde 1346 – mittlerweile konnte sich wieder eine kleine Gemeinde etablieren – erhoben. Herzog Ludwig der Bayer verhinderte ein Pogrom, aber schon drei Jahre später war die Jüdische Gemeinde von einer *zweiten Katastrophe* betroffen: Die in ganz Mitteleuropa wütenden Pestverfolgungen ergriffen auch München, abermals waren es Münchner Bürger, die die Jüdische Gemeinde vernichteten.

Zwei Jahrzehnte später, um 1360, bildete sich erneut ein jüdisches Gemeinwesen, und um 1380 deuten die Errichtung von Synagoge und Hospital in der Judengasse auf dem Areal des heutigen Marienhofs auf ein blühendes Gemeindeleben hin.

1442 erlebte die mittelalterliche Jüdische Gemeinde ihre *dritte Katastrophe*, die Vertreibung aus der Stadt durch Herzog Albrecht III. und ein darauf folgendes, fast 300 Jahre andauerndes Verbot des Aufenthalts in München und ganz Altbayern.

Erst im frühen 18. Jahrhundert gestattete der Hof einigen privilegierten Juden aus den süddeutschen Landgemeinden um Augsburg die zeitweilige Niederlassung in

A further 13th-century source does not just provide a more profound view of the first Jewish community in Munich in the Middle Ages, but at the same time is testimony to the *first catastrophe*—the pogrom of 1285, during which at least sixty-eight Jews were slain by Christians from Munich or burned to death in their synagogue, their names being recorded in the *Memorbuch* of the Jewish community in Nuremberg. The accusation that Jews murdered a Christian boy for ritual purposes allegedly triggered off this pogrom. The same accusation was made again in 1346 against the small community that had, in the meantime, re-established itself. Duke Ludwig the Bavarian prevented one pogrom, but just three years later the Jewish community was hit by a *second catastrophe*: the persecution of individuals or groups of people that accompanied the spread of the Plague across the whole of central Europe, also reached Munich where, once again, it was the citizens of Munich who annihilated the Jewish community.

Some fourteen years later, around 1360, a Jewish community had re-emerged and the construction of a synagogue and a hostipal in the "Judengasse" (Jews' Alley) on the site of what is today Marienhof, would suggest that the community was flourishing.

In 1442 the Jewish community of the Middle Ages experienced its *third catastrophe*: its expulsion from the city by Duke Albrecht III and a ban on living in Munich and the whole of the region of Old Bavaria, which was to last almost 300 years.

Only in the early 18th century were the court's own privileged Jews, from the rural communities of southern Germany around Augsburg, granted temporary residency.

München. Hofjuden wie die Mändles, Wertheimer oder Oppenheimer wurden als Geldgeber für die immer aufwändiger werdende Hofführung benötigt, was ihnen das Recht eines vorübergehenden Aufenthalts einbrachte. In mehreren Weinschenken „Im Tal" entstand um 1750 ein bescheidenes jüdisches Zentrum, zu dem auch eine kleine Betstube – die erste Synagoge seit der Vertreibung 1442 – gehörte. In der zweiten Hälfte des 18. Jahrhunderts bildete sich aus dieser kleinen, mit Aufenthaltsprivilegien ausgestatteten Gruppe durch den Zuzug von Familienangehörigen und Dienstboten eine jüdische Gemeinde, die 1815 im Zuge der seit dem späten 18. Jahrhundert einsetzenden Emanzipation als „Israelitische Kultusgemeinde München" ihren gesetzlichen und organisatorischen Rahmen erhielt. 1826 erfolgte der – noch hinter einer gewöhnlichen Hausfassade versteckte – Bau der Synagoge, die mit ihren über 300 Sitzplätzen der wachsenden Gemeinde Raum für ihre Gottesdienste bot.

Mit der Gründung des Deutschen Reichs 1871 wurden die Münchner Juden zu gleichberechtigten Staatsbürgern. Dieses Jahr ist der Beginn einer Epoche, die 62 Jahre andauern und den Münchner Juden erstmals ein gleichberechtigtes und freies Leben in der Stadt ermöglichen sollte. Der Bau von zwei Synagogen 1887 und 1892 und die Mitwirkung von Juden, die sich nun „Deutsche Staatsbürger jüdischen Glaubens" nannten, an Wirtschaft, Kultur und Gesellschaftsleben Münchens markieren eine glückliche Epoche. Mit über 11.000 Mitgliedern erreichte die Israelitische Kultusgemeinde 1911 auch demografisch ihren Zenit.

The services of Court Jews such as the Mändles, Wertheimers, and Oppenheimers were required as moneylenders to meet the increasingly extravagant costs of holding court. This brought with it the right of abode, albeit not permanent. A modest center of Jewish life became established around 1750 in the wine taverns in the street "Im Tal." This also included a small prayer room—the first synagogue since the Jews' expulsion in 1442. In the second half of the 18th century, this small group, which enjoyed the privilege of residency and had now been joined by family members and servants who had moved to the city, evolved into a Jewish community. In 1815 it gained a legal and organisational form as the "Israelitische Kultusgemeinde München" (Jewish Religious Community of Munich) as a result of the emancipatory thinking that came about in the late 18th century. In 1826 a synagogue was built, although it remained hidden behind the façade of a normal house. With seating for 300, it offered the growing community enough space to hold their religious services.

With the founding of the German Reich in 1871, the Jews of Munich also became citizens with the same rights as everybody else. This year marked the beginning of a new era that would last sixty-two years, during which—for the first time in the city's history—Jews in Munich enjoyed a life without any restrictions and on an equal footing with other citizens. The building of two synagogues in 1887 and 1892, and the participation of Jews—who now called themselves "German citizens of Jewish faith"— in the economical, cultural, and social life of Munich, were signs of a harmonious era. With more than 11,000 members, the Jewish Religious Community also reached its heyday in 1911.

Der 30. Januar 1933, die Machtergreifung durch die Nationalsozialisten, markiert den Beginn der *vierten Katastrophe* für die Münchner Juden. Sukzessive grenzte die sich zum Nationalsozialismus bekennende Mehrheit Münchens Juden aus, entzog ihnen die Existenzgrundlage und profitierte von deren Ausbeutung. Nach der Pogromnacht vom 9. November 1938 mündete diese Verfolgung in die nationalsozialistische Vernichtungspolitik, an deren Ende die Vertreibung von rund 7.000 und die Ermordung von über 3.000 Münchner Jüdinnen und Juden standen.

Nach 1945 war München für wenige Jahre ein Zentrum für jene Überlebenden vornehmlich aus Osteuropa, die hier auf ihre Weiterreise nach Israel, Nordamerika und andere Länder warteten. Einige von ihnen blieben in München und bildeten mit den wenigen, die in München überlebt hatten oder aus der Emigration zurückkehrten, die Nachkriegsgemeinde. Der 1990 einsetzende Zuzug von Juden aus den Ländern der ehemaligen Sowjetunion stellte neue Herausforderungen an die bis dahin im Verborgenen wirkende Kultusgemeinde, die im Bau des Jüdischen Zentrums am St.-Jakobs-Platz ihren auch nach außen hin deutlich sichtbaren Ausdruck fanden. Die in den 1990er Jahren erfolgte Gründung der Reformgemeinde „Beth Shalom" ist schließlich als Hinweis auf eine zunehmende Pluralität innerhalb der jüdischen Gemeinschaft Münchens zu verstehen.

Anders als die Dauerausstellung „Stimmen_Orte_Zeiten" des Jüdischen Museums will die Ausstellung „Stadt ohne Juden" nun nicht jenen Jahren in Münchens Geschichte nachspüren, in denen jüdische Münchner in dieser Stadt lebten und

January 30, 1933, the day the National Socialists seized power, marked the beginning of the *fourth catastrophe* for Munich's Jews. The majority of Munich's residents, which had avowed itself to National Socialism, gradually excluded the Jews, took away their means of livelihood, and profited from their exploitation. After *Kristallnacht* of November 9, 1938, this persecution culminated in the National Socialists' policy of extermination, leading to the expulsion of some 7,000 Munich Jews and the murder of more than 3,000.

For a few years after 1945, Munich became a center for those survivors, largely from eastern Europe, who were waiting to travel on to Israel, North America, and other countries. Some stayed in Munich and, together with the few who had survived the War in Munich or had returned from emigration, built up the post-war community. The religious congregation, which had largely kept itself out of public view, faced a new challenge, which began in 1990 with the arrival of Jews from countries in the former Soviet Union, and which was to find its clearly visible expression to the world in the building of the Jewish Center on St. Jakobs Platz. The founding of the "Beth Shalom" reform congregation in the 1990s is ultimately to be seen as sign of an increasing plurality within the Jewish community in Munich.

As a contrast to the permanent exhibition "Voices_Places_Times" at the Jewish Museum Munich, "City without Jews" does not trace the years in Munich's history when Jews lived in and helped shape the city, but looks at the gaps caused by the four catastrophes which have plagued Munich's Jews over the past 850 years; gaps that amount to more than 400 years, during which Jewish life in Munich was not possible.

sie mitgestalteten, sondern jene Leerstellen aufzeigen, die mit den vier Katastrophen, von denen die Juden Münchens in den vergangenen 850 Jahren betroffen waren, verbunden sind und die sich auf über 400 Jahre addieren, in denen jüdisches Leben in München nicht möglich waren.

Die Ausstellung des Jüdischen Museums, die wie immer dem Prinzip der Reduktion verpflichtet ist, versammelt zwölf Exponate, die ein Licht auf diese Epochen einer „Stadt ohne Juden" werfen und zugleich Einblicke geben, wie Vorurteile, Legenden und Gerüchte über Juden von der Mehrheitsgesellschaft in diesen Zeitabschnitten rezipiert wurden. Am Anfang steht mit dem „Nürnberger Memorbuch" (*Kat. Nr. 1*) ein Dokument jüdischer Erinnerungskultur, mit dem die Überlebenden der Pogrome des ausgehenden 13. Jahrhunderts auch den Münchner Märtyrern gedachten. Die weiteren Objekte der Ausstellung stehen überwiegend mit der Erinnerungskultur der Mehrheitsgesellschaft in Verbindung, die Vorurteile und Stereotypen über Juden über Generationen überlieferte. Bildliche Darstellungen der angeblichen Ritualmorde von 1285 und 1346 (*Kat. Nr. 2*) wurden noch im 17. und 18. Jahrhundert verbreitet. Ein im Zusammenhang mit dem Pogrom von 1349 erhobener Vorwurf des Hostienfrevels führte zu einem Kult, der eine Kapelle, steinerne Gedenksäulen und – fast 300 Jahre später – ein Altarbild (*Kat. Nr. 3*) entstehen ließ, das bis in das 19. Jahrhundert den Vorwurf, Juden seien Gottesmörder, tradierte. Dieses 1624 entstandene und in den vergangenen Jahrzehnten in Vergessenheit geratene Tafelbild, das im Zuge der Ausstellungsvorbereitungen im Domschatz der Münchner Frauenkirche entdeckt wurde und

The exhibition focuses on just twelve exhibits which throw light on these periods in a "city without Jews," while at the same time looking at the prejudices, legends, and rumors about Jews that were nurtured by the majority of people at those times. The exhibition starts with the "Nuremberg *Memorbuch*" (*cat. no. 1*), a document of the Jewish culture of remembrance with which the survivors of the pogrom at the end of the 13th century honored those residents of Munich who suffered a martyr's death. The other objects in the exhibition are largely associated with the culture of remembrance adopted by the majority of society, and the prejudices and stereotypical views of Jews passed down from one generation to the next. Pictures of the alleged ritual murders committed in 1285 and 1346 (*cat. no. 2*) became widespread in the 17th and 18th centuries. The reputed desecration of the Host connected with the pogrom of 1349 led to a cult which saw the building of a chapel, stone memorial columns, and—almost 300 years later—the painting of an altarpiece (*cat. no. 3*), that kept the accusation alive well into the 19th century that Jews were responsible for the murder of Christ. This painting of 1624, long forgotten over the past few decades and found in the Treasury of the Frauenkirche (Church of Our Lady) in Munich during preparatory work on this exhibition, is shown here within its historical context for the first time, and can well be considered the most important historical object that has come to light within the past few decades related to the history of the persecution of Jews in Munich.

A Gothic sculpture, which at first glance would seem to be an unusual object to have in an exhibition in a Jewish museum, is directly connected with the expulsion of the Jews in 1442. This larger than life-sized sculpture, now known as the "Salmdorfer *Pietà*" (*cat. no. 4*), is one of the most important depictions of the mourning Virgin Mary

nun erstmals in seinem historischen Kontext vorgestellt wird, darf als die wohl wichtigste Wiederentdeckung eines historischen Objekts zur Geschichte der Verfolgung der Juden in München in den letzten Jahrzehnten bezeichnet werden.

Mit der Vertreibung von 1442 in direktem Zusammenhang steht eine gotische Plastik, die auf den ersten Blick ein ungewohntes Exponat für eine Ausstellung eines Jüdischen Museums ist. Das heute unter dem Namen „Salmdorfer Pietà" bekannte, überlebensgroße Vesperbild (*Kat. Nr. 4*) zählt zu den bedeutendsten Darstellungen der „Schmerzhaften Gottesmutter" des Hochmittelalters. Nachdem die Synagoge der vertriebenen Gemeinde nach 1442 in eine Kirche umgewandelt worden war, wurde sie – als Zeichen des Sieges der Ecclesia über die Synagoga – zum Gegenstand christlicher Verehrung.

Weitere Exponate spüren der judenfeindlichen Politik Herzog Albrechts V. (*Kat. Nr. 5*), die 1553 zu einer Erneuerung des Aufenthaltsverbots für Juden im Herzogtum Bayern führte, der in München immer wiederkehrenden Legende von Ahasver, dem „Ewigen Juden" (*Kat. Nr. 6*), den ersten, prekären Aufenthaltsmöglichkeiten von Hofjuden wie Samuel Wolf Wertheimer (*Kat. Nr. 7*) und der Hoffnung vieler Juden, durch die Taufe, den Übertritt vom Judentum zum Christentum (*Kat. Nr. 8*), an den Bürgerrechten teilhaben zu können, nach.

Ein Vorbote und Wegbereiter der Schoa war der in der 2. Hälfte des 19. Jahrhunderts aufkeimende rassistische Antisemitismus, den sich auch weite Kreise

of the Late Middle Ages. When the synagogue was converted into a church following the expulsion of the Jews in 1442, the *Pietà* were seen as a sign of the victory of *Ecclesia* over *Synagoga*, and became the object of Christian veneration.

Other exhibits trace the anti-Jewish politics of Duke Albrecht V (*cat. no. 5*), which led to a renewal of the prohibition for Jews to settle in the Duchy of Bavaria in 1553; the legend that is often retold in Munich of Ahasver, the "Wandering Jew" (*cat. no. 6*); the first precarious possibility that Court Jews such as Samuel Wolf Wertheimer had to reside in the city (*cat. no. 7*); and the hope that many Jews nurtured of being able to enjoy common civil rights by being baptised and converting from Judaism to Christianity (*cat. no. 8*).

The racist anti-Semitism that started to emerge in the second half of the 19th century, and that was adopted by wide sections of the Catholic church, was a harbinger and precursor of the Shoah. One of the most vehement representatives of this approach to anti-Semitism, which urged the complete exclusion of Jews from society, was the Catholic priest and Member of Parliament Georg Ratzinger, who extolled his demands in publications (*cat. no. 9*) and parliamentary speeches.

To render visible the gaping hole left by the years from 1933 to 1945 with just one single exhibit, is impossible. The empty trunk (*cat. no. 10*), that belonged to the Jew Rosa Picard of Munich, can only stand as a symbol for the murder of more than 3,000 Jews from Munich during the Shoah.

der katholischen Kirche zu eigen machten. Einer der vehementesten Vertreter dieser Richtung, die auf eine völlige Ausgrenzung jüdischer Bürger drängte, war der katholische Priester und Parlamentsabgeordnete Georg Ratzinger, der seine Ausgrenzungsforderungen in Veröffentlichungen (*Kat. Nr. 9*) und Landtagsreden erhob.

Die Leerstelle, welche die Jahre 1933–1945 hinterließen, mit einem einzigen Exponat zu visualisieren, ist unmöglich. Der leere Überseekoffer der Münchner Jüdin Rosa Picard (*Kat. Nr. 10*) kann deshalb nur unzulänglicher Verweis auf die Ermordung von über 3.000 Münchner Juden während der Schoa sein.

Für die ersten Nachkriegsjahre, die Zeit, als München eine „Durchgangsstation" für Überlebende auf ihrer Weiterreise in die Freiheit war, steht ein Seder-Teller aus dem Jahr 1947 (*Kat. Nr. 11*), dessen Inschrift den traditionellen Pessach-Wunsch „*Nächstes* Jahr in Jerusalem!" in das eindringliche Postulat „*Dieses* Jahr in Jerusalem!" umformuliert. Als letztes der zwölf Exponate ruft die 1990 von den Künstlern Rudolf Herz und Thomas Lehnerer an der Feldherrnhalle als demokratisches Denk- und Mahnmal befestigte Tafel mit der Inschrift „Juden in aller Welt bitte kommt zurück, wenn Ihr wollt!" (*Kat. Nr. 12*) die Verpflichtung der Zivilgesellschaft in Erinnerung, Verantwortung zu übernehmen.

Den zwölf Exponaten, die überwiegend negative Ereignisse der Stadtgeschichte visualisieren, sind in der Ausstellung Videotafeln zugeordnet. Studierende der Hochschule für Fernsehen und Film München haben Statements von Historikern,

A *Seder* plate of 1947 (*cat. no. 11*), which instead of the traditional Passover wish "*Next* year in Jerusalem," bears the striking postulate "*This* year in Jerusalem," represents the period directly after the end of the War, a time in which Munich was a "stop-over point" for Jewish survivors on their onward journey to a freedom they so longed for.

The last of the twelve exhibits, the sign fixed by the artists Rudolf Herz and Thomas Lehnerer to the Feldherrnhalle (Field Marshals' Hall) in 1990 as a democratic memorial and monument, bearing the inscription "Jews from around the world, please come back, if you want to" (*cat. no. 12*), is a reminder of our civil duty to assume responsibility.

The twelve exhibits, which render predominantly negative events in the city's history visible, are complemented by video boards in the exhibition. Students at the University for Television and Film Munich have collated statements by historians and experts in the fields of literature, politics, and cultural affairs, related to Munich's topography and which refer to events of exclusion, persecution, and annihilation that actually happened. This allows visitors to the exhibition "City without Jews—The Dark Side of Munich's History" to see the objects in a broader historical context while at the same time linking them to specific sites in Munich.

Literatur-, Politik- und Kulturwissenschaftlern in Bezug zu den Orten in der Topographie Münchens gestellt, die mit den konkreten Ereignissen von Ausgrenzung, Vertreibung und Vernichtung in Zusammenhang stehen. Den Besucherinnen und Besuchern der Ausstellung „Stadt ohne Juden – Die Nachtseite der Münchner Stadtgeschichte" ermöglicht dies, die Exponate in einen breiteren Kontext der Geschichte zu stellen und gleichzeitig mit konkreten Orten in München in Verbindung zu bringen.

Das Münchner Jubeljahr 2008 markiert auch ein besonderes Ereignis in der fast 850 Jahre andauernden jüdischen Geschichte der Stadt: Seit 63 Jahren – so lange dauert die gerne als „Nachkriegszeit" bezeichnete Epoche an – können Jüdinnen und Juden in München in Freiheit und Unabhängigkeit leben. Damit vermessen die Jahrzehnte seit 1945 den längsten Zeitabschnitt in der Geschichte Münchens, in dem ein gesellschaftlicher Konsens darüber besteht, dass Bürgerrechte und Menschenrechte unteilbar sind und Juden so wie andere religiöse oder ethnische Gruppen ein integraler Bestandteil der Stadtgesellschaft sind. Doch diese gesellschaftliche Übereinkunft ist nicht unverbrüchlich: Auch in den letzten Jahrzehnten war jüdisches Leben in München bedroht. Das nie aufgeklärte Attentat auf das Jüdische Altersheim von 1970 mit sieben Todesopfern, das Olympia-Massaker von 1972 mit elf Ermordeten, die Attentatspläne deutscher Neonazis bei der Grundsteinlegung des Jüdischen Zentrums am St.-Jakobs-Platz 2003, aber auch der tägliche Antisemitismus, der in anonymen Briefen und offenen Äußerungen an den Tag tritt, zeigen, dass auch heute die Münchner Stadtgesellschaft nicht zur Gänze dagegen gefeit ist, so zu versagen, wie sie es in der 850-jährigen Geschichte häufig getan hat, und deshalb Verantwortung trägt.

Munich's anniversary in 2008 also marks a special occasion in the almost 850-year-old Jewish history of the city. For sixty-three years—for the duration of the so-called postwar era—Jews have been able to live in liberty and independence. Seen in this light, the years since 1945 represent the longest period in the history of Munich in which a social consensus has existed that civil and human rights are indivisible, and that Jews—like other religious or ethnic groups—form an integral part of the city's society. This social accord is not however inviolable: even in the past few decades Jewish life in Munich has been under threat. The attack on the Jewish home for the elderly in 1970, which left seven dead, has never been solved; the massacre during the Olympic Games in 1972 with eleven victims; the planned attack by German neo-Nazis during the ceremony to lay the foundation stone for the Jewish Center on St. Jakobs Platz in 2003; and everyday anti-Semitism in the form of anonymous letters and statements made in public that come to light—all these go to show that even today the people of Munich are not entirely immune from failing in the same way as has so often been the case during the city's 850-year history, and that they must therefore continue to be aware of their responsibility.

Katalog
catalogue

Ritualmord-Vorwurf und Pogrom 1285

Mit Abraham „dem Municher" lässt sich 1229 erstmals ein Jude in der im Jahr 1158 gegründeten Stadt München nachweisen. Schriftliche Hinweise auf eine jüdische Gemeinde bleiben in den folgenden Jahrzehnten spärlich. Erst Nachrichten über die Vernichtung der Münchner Juden im Jahr 1285 lassen Rückschlüsse auf die Größe der Gemeinde zu.

Im Herbst 1285 machte in der Stadt das Gerücht die Runde, Juden hätten ein christliches Kind ermordet, um dessen Blut für rituelle Zwecke zu nutzen. Am 12. Oktober überfielen Christen die in der Synagoge versammelten Juden und boten jenen, die zur Taufe bereit wären, freies Geleit. Da kein Einziger der Bedrängten auf dieses Angebot einging, setzten die Christen die Synagoge in Brand; die darin befindlichen Juden – ihre Zahl wird unterschiedlich mit 68 bis 187 beziffert – fanden als Märtyrer den Tod.

Die Namen von 68 Opfern wurden 1296 in ein neu angelegtes Memorbuch der Jüdischen Gemeinde Nürnberg eingetragen. Dessen Nekrologium, ein Verzeichnis von bei Pogromen Ermordeter, listet Hunderte von Städten auf, in denen es zu Judenverfolgungen kam, und nennt für viele dieser Orte auch die Namen der Opfer. Diese Namen wurden zweimal im Jahr, am Schabbat vor dem Feiertag Schawuot (Wochenfest) und am Schabbat vor dem 9. Av, dem Trauer- und Gedenktag an die Tempelzerstörung, in der Synagoge vorgelesen.

Als es 1348/49 abermals zu Pogromen kam, war die Zahl der Opfer so groß, dass ihre Namen nicht mehr in das Memorbuch eingetragen werden konnten und stattdessen stellvertretend die Namen von 124 vernichteten Gemeinden – darunter auch München – in das Nekrologium aufgenommen wurden.

Das Nürnberger Memorbuch gelangte im 15. Jahrhundert an die Synagoge von Mainz, befand sich vorübergehend in Privatbesitz und wurde im 19. Jahrhundert von der Jüdischen Gemeinde Mainz zurückgekauft. 1898 wurde es vom Mainzer Rabbiner Sigmund Salfeld ediert. Seit der Schoa ist über seinen Verbleib nichts bekannt. Möglicherweise befindet es sich heute in englischem Privatbesitz.

[B.Pu.]

Accusations of Ritual Murder and Pogrom in 1285

The first mention of a Jew living in the city of Munich, founded in 1158, was Abraham "the Municher" in 1229. Written evidence of a Jewish community in the decades to follow however remains scant. Only news about the annihilation of Munich's Jews in 1285 allows conclusions to be drawn about the size of the congregation.

In Fall 1285, a rumor spread throughout the city that a Jew had murdered a Christian child so that its blood could be used in a ritual. On October 12, Christians attacked the Jews assembled in the synagogue and offered to set those free who were prepared to be baptised. Since none of the besieged took up this offer, the Christians set fire to the synagogue. The Jews caught inside—and here the numbers vary from 68 to 187—suffered a martyr's death.

In 1296, the names of 68 victims were entered in a *Memorbuch* that had recently been created for the Jewish community in Nuremberg. Its necrologium—a list of names of those murdered in pogroms against Jews—includes hundreds of towns in which the persecution of Jews had taken place, and in many instances lists the names of victims. These names were read out twice a year, on the Sabbath before the Jewish holiday *Shavuot* (the Festival of Weeks) and on the Sabbath before *Tisha B'Av*, that commemorates the destruction of the temples in Jerusalem.

When it came to a resurgence of pogroms in 1348/49, the number of victims was so great that not all names could be entered in the *Memorbuch*; instead, the names of 124 communities that had been annihilated, including Munich, were listed in the necrologium.

The Nuremberg *Memorbuch* came into the possession of the synagogue in Mainz in the 15th century; for a brief period it went into private ownership before being bought back by the Jewish community in Mainz in the 19th century. In 1898 it was edited by Rabbi Sigmund Salfeld of Mainz. Since the *Shoah*, its whereabouts in unknown. It is possible that is in a private collection in England.

„Die Memorbücher der jüdischen Gemeinden in Deutschland stellen die älteste Überlieferung der schriftlich-liturgischen Form des Gedenkens an Verstorbene im Judentum dar. Die ältesten dieser Handschriften gehen auf das späte 13. Jahrhundert zurück, aber erst gegen Ende des 16. Jahrhunderts setzte sich die Verwendung dieser Handschriften durch. Als Verzeichnisse sowohl individueller wie auch kollektiver Formen des Gedenkens und der Erinnerung sind sie heute eine wichtige Quelle für lokalgeschichtliche und sozial- und religionsgeschichtliche Forschungen wie auch für die Familienforschung."

"The Memorbücher of the German Jewish communities represent the oldest transmission of the lithurgic literary form of the memorialization of the dead in Judaism. The earliest such manuscript appeared at the end of the 13th century but it was only towards the end of the 16th century that these manuscripts became widespread. As record of both individual and collective forms of memorialization and remembrance they serve as important sources for local, social and religious history as well as for genealogical research."

Aubrey Pomerance
Historiker \ Historian

1

Das Martyrologium des Nürnberger Memorbuches
herausgegeben von
Dr. Siegmund Salfeld
Berlin, 1898
Druck
gr. 8°

Jüdisches Museum
München

1

The Martyrology of the Nuremberg Memorbuch
edited by
Dr. Siegmund Salfeld
Berlin, 1898
Print
gr. 8°

Jewish Museum
Munich

Ritualmord-Vorwurf 1346

Der gegen Juden erhobene Vorwurf des Ritualmordes – also die Anschuldigung, Juden würden zur Osterzeit den Gottesmord an einem Christenkind wiederholen – ist ein seit dem 12. Jahrhundert europaweit zu verzeichnendes Phänomen. Für das 13. und 14. Jahrhundert sind auch für München zwei dieser Legenden bekannt.

Der Kupferstich greift die Legende vom Knaben Heinrich auf, der 1346 außerhalb der Stadtmauern tot aufgefunden wurde. Das in Umlauf gebrachte Gerücht besagte, dass der Junge von Juden erstochen worden sei, die sein Blut für rituelle Zwecke verwenden wollten. Nahe dem Fundort in der Gegend des heutigen Karolinenplatzes wurden Andachtskapellen und ein Kreuz zum Gedenken an den Knaben aufgestellt.

Johannes von Winterthur (um 1300 – um 1348) berichtet in seiner Chronik als Erster über den Vorwurf. Ein zweiter Bericht, der den Ritualmord-Vorwurf aufgreift, stammt aus dem 16. Jahrhundert von Johannes Aventinus. Allerdings datiert dieser den Ritualmord ein Jahr früher als Winterthur. Ungeachtet dieser Unstimmigkeit ist die Kontinuität beachtlich, mit der sich der Ritualmord-Vorwurf durch die Geschichte Münchens zieht.

Die Legende war in der Bevölkerung stets präsent. So wurde der angebliche Fundort des Knaben noch Jahrhunderte später „Bei der Kindsmarter" genannt. Auch zeitlich folgende Chroniken griffen die Legende immer wieder auf und bestärkten damit das Misstrauen gegenüber Juden, welches meist mit dem Wunsch nach deren Ausgrenzung einherging.

In diesem Kontext wurde auch der Kupferstich von Jeremias Kilian angefertigt, der erstmals in der 1615 bis 1627 veröffentlichten Sammlung von Heiligenlegenden „Bavaria Sancta" mit lateinischem Begleittext abgedruckt wurde. Ein knappes Jahrhundert später, im Jahr 1714, wurde der Kupferstich einem breiteren Publikum durch die deutsche Übersetzung der „Bavaria Sancta" unter dem Titel „Heiliges Bayer-Land" bekannt gemacht.

Die Ritualmord-Legenden schürten den Antijudaismus in der christlichen Bevölkerung und hatten vielerorts Pogrome zur Folge. Der Umstand, dass es sich bei den Anschuldigungen um unbelegbare Vorwürfe handelte, schmälerte das Ausmaß der Legendenverbreitung und den damit einhergehenden Antijudaismus wie Antisemitismus nicht. Noch bis ins 20. Jahrhundert wurde in Europa der angeblichen Ritualmord-Opfer als Märtyrer gedacht.

[T.Ne.]

Accusation of Ritual Murder in 1346

The accusation that Jews committed ritual murders—and that a Christian child would be murdered in God's name every Easter—has been a phenomenon chronicled since the 12th century throughout Europe. Two such legends from the 13th and 14th centuries were known in Munich.

The copperplate engraving takes up the legend of the young boy Heinrich, who was found dead in 1346 outside the city walls. The rumor that was started told of the boy being stabbed to death by Jews who wanted his blood for ritual purposes. Near where his body was found, in the area around what is now Karolinenplatz, memorial chapels and a cross in memory of the boy were erected.

Johannes von Winterthur (c. 1300–c. 1348) was the first to report on this accusation in his chronicle. A second report which picked up on the alleged ritual murder, came from Johannes Aventinus in the 16th century, although his version puts the date of the murder one year earlier. Irrespective of this discrepancy, it is remarkable how accusations of ritual murder were perpetuated throughout Munich's history.

Such legends were firmly implanted in the minds of those living here. This resulted in the place where the boy was supposedly found being renamed "Bei der Kindsmarter" (Near the Martyred Child) even centuries later. Subsequent chronicles also reiterated these legends again and again and intensified the mistrust of Jews, frequently accompanied by the wish to ostracise them.

It was also in this context that Jeremias Kilian made this engraving which was first printed in *Bavaria Sancta*, a collection of religious legends accompanied by texts in Latin, published between 1615 and 1627. Almost a century later, in 1714, the engraving became known to a much broader public following the translation of *Bavaria Sancta*, which appeared as *Heiliges Bayer-Land* (The Holy Land of Bavaria).

Legends about ritual murders fueled anti-Jewish sentiments among the Christian population and led to pogroms in many places. The fact that such accusations were unproven allegations hindered neither the spread of legends nor feelings against Judaism and anti-Semitism. The alleged victim of this ritual murder was still remembered in Europe right into the 20th century.

„Der Ritualmord-Vorwurf gegen Juden hat sich im Mittelalter seit dem 12. Jahrhundert von England über Frankreich, Deutschland, Italien ausgebreitet wie eine nie enden wollende Epidemie. Die Vorwürfe, die gegen die Juden vorgebracht wurden, waren, sie bräuchten Christenblut für magische, aber auch für religiöse Zwecke. Das Ganze steht im Zusammenhang mit der Vorstellung der christlichen Theologie, die Juden seien Gottesmörder und sie hätten den Wunsch, immer wieder, insbesondere in der Passionszeit, christliche Knaben umzubringen, um auf diese Weise den Tod Jesu Christi noch einmal nachzuvollziehen."

"Ever since the 12th century, accusations of ritual murder against Jews spread from England to France, Germany, and Italy in the Middle Ages like a never-ending epidemic. The accusations brought against the Jews were that they needed the blood of Christians for sorcery as well as for religious rituals. This was all related to the notion in Christian theology that Jews were responsible for the killing of Jesus and that, time and again—and especially during the second half of Lent—they wanted to murder Christian boys to re-enact Christ's death."

Winfried Frey
Literaturhistoriker
\ Literary Historian

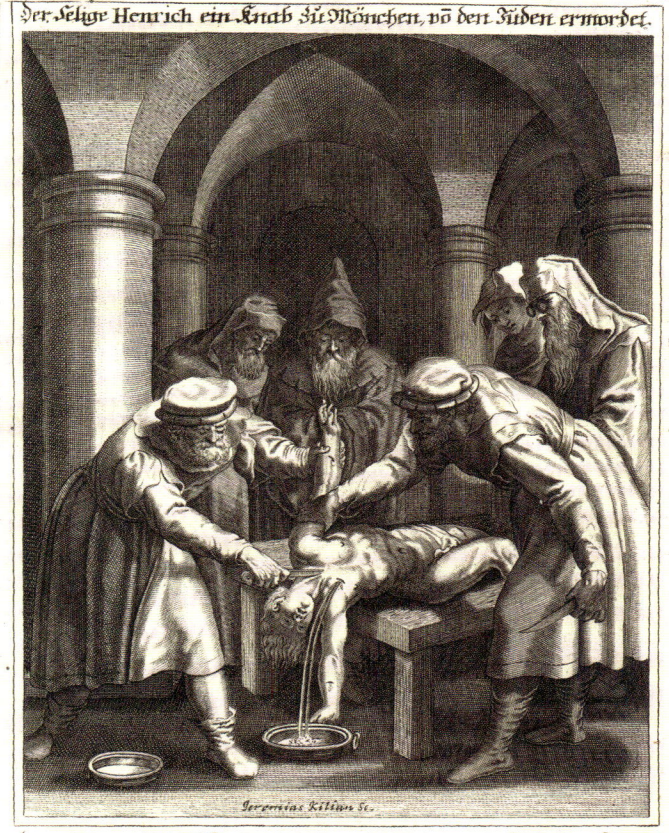

2
Der Selige Henrich ein Knab zu Mönchen, von den Juden ermordet
Jeremias Kilian (1665–1730)
Kupferstich
aus: Matthäus Rader: Heiliges Bayer-Land, übersetzt von Maximilian Rassler
Augsburg, 1714
H: 22 cm, B: 15 cm

Jüdisches Museum München, # JM 10/2008

2
The Blessed Henrich, a boy of Munich, murdered by the Jews
Jeremias Kilian (1665–1730)
Copperplate engraving
from: Matthäus Rader: Heiliges Bayer-Land, translated by Maximilian Rassler
Augsburg, 1714
H: 22 cm, W: 15 cm

Jewish Museum Munich, # JM 10/2008

Hostienfrevel-Beschuldigung 1349

Das Vierte Laterankonzil legte 1215 die Lehre der Transsubstantiation fest. Sie besagt, dass sich bei der Eucharistie Brot und Wein in das Fleisch und Blut Christi verwandeln. Den Gläubigen wurde diese Vorstellung durch Legenden von Hostienwundern und Hostienfreveln nähergebracht.

In München verbreitete sich seit dem 14. Jahrhundert die Legende, Juden hätten eine christliche Frau dafür bezahlt, eine geweihte Hostie beiseitezuschaffen und ihnen zu überbringen, um diese Hostie zu malträtieren und so das Leiden Christi wiederholen zu können. Vor dem Schwabinger Tor (am heutigen Odeonsplatz) soll die Frau jedoch gefasst und die Hostie in einer feierlichen Prozession zurück in die Frauenkirche gebracht worden sein.

Die Überlieferung nennt unterschiedliche Jahreszahlen für diesen angeblichen Vorfall. Am ehesten dürfte die Legende mit der Pest-Verfolgung im Jahr 1349 zusammenhängen, als die Münchner Juden teilweise ermordet, teilweise vertrieben wurden. Ritualmord- und Hostienfrevel-Vorwürfe wurden vielfach nachträglich als Rechtfertigung von Verfolgungen herangezogen. Darauf deutet auch die Errichtung einer Kapelle zu Ehren Christi als Heiler der Welt („Salvator") vor dem Schwabinger Tor 1350 hin, da die Gründung von Salvatorkirchen häufig mit solchen Legenden in Verbindung steht. Nach Abbruch der Kapelle 1493 stand bis in das späte 18. Jahrhundert an ihrer Stelle eine steinerne Gedenksäule mit der Darstellung des „sakrilegischen Weibs".

Fast 200 Jahre nach der Vertreibung der Münchner Juden stiftete die Bürgerstochter Ursula Meyrin im Jahr 1624 für die neue, 1494 innerhalb der Stadtmauern errichtete Salvatorkirche dieses Tafelbild, dessen nicht mehr erhaltene Stifterinschrift die Legende nacherzählt. Vor der architektonisch überhöhten Kulisse des Schwabinger Tors stellt das Simultanbild den angeblichen Frevel in drei Szenen dar: Sie zeigen drei Juden mit der bis ins 16. Jahrhundert verpflichtenden Kennzeichnung („Gelber Fleck"), die Ergreifung der Frau und schließlich die feierliche Rückführung der Hostie.

Nach der Säkularisierung der Salvatorkirche 1803 gelangte das Tafelbild in die Frauenkirche und hielt dort bis in das späte 19. Jahrhundert die Erinnerung an den angeblichen Hostienfrevel durch Münchner Juden im 14. Jahrhundert wach.

[B.Pu.]

Accusation of Host Desecration in 1349

In 1215, the Fourth Lateran Council laid down the doctrine of transsubstantiation, stating that, in the Eucharist, the bread and wine are changed into the Body and Blood of Christ. The faithful were taught to understand this by tales about miracles and the desecration of the Host.

Since the 14th century in Munich, a legend had been running rife about Jews who had paid a Christian woman to steal a Host for them that had already been blessed, so that they could abuse it and thus repeat the Suffering of Christ. Outside Schwabing Gate (on what is today Odeonsplatz) the woman was caught and the Host returned to the Frauenkirche in a ceremonious procession.

Traditionally, different dates are given for this occurrence. The earliest would appear to be the legend associated with the Plague-related persecution in 1349, at which time some Jews in Munich were murdered while others were driven out. Accusations of ritual murder and Host desecration were frequently given as a means of justifying persecution after the event. The building of a chapel to honor Christ as the Savior of the World ("Salvator") outside Schwabing Gate in 1350 would also suggest that this is the case, especially as the founding of churches dedicated to the Savior were often linked to such legends. After the chapel was demolished in 1493, a stone column with a depiction of the "sacrilegious woman" stood on the site until the late 18th century.

Almost 200 years later, in 1624, following the expulsion of the Jews from Munich, the burgher's daughter Ursual Meyrin donated this painting on panel to the new Salvator Church that had been erected in 1494 within the city walls. The donor's inscription, which no longer exists, retold the legend. Against an exaggerated architectural depiction of Schwabing Gate, three scenes relating the alleged desecration are shown simultaneously in this painting: They include three Jews with their identifying yellow badges that had to be worn until the mid 16th century, the capturing of the woman, and the festive return of the Host.

Following the secularisation of the Salvator Church in 1803, the painting was kept in the Frauenkirche (Church of Our Lady) and the memory of this alleged desecration of the Host by the Jews of Munich was kept alive right up until the late 19th century.

„Wir finden vorwiegend seit dem 13. Jahrhundert durch das ganze Hochmittelalter hindurch Hostienfrevel-Geschichten, in denen sich Juden unrechtmäßig eine Hostie beschafft haben und an dieser Hostie die Marter Christi erneut vollzogen haben sollen. Sie sollen diese Hostie mit Nägeln gestochen oder mit Messern traktiert haben, bis schließlich aus dieser Hostie Blut geflossen sein soll, was dann ja auch ein Beweis für diese Lehre der Transsubstantiation wäre."

"Legends about the desecration of the Host are predominantly found from the 13th century onward right through the whole of High Middle Ages, which tell of Jews getting hold of the Host and allegedly bringing about a repeat of the Suffering of Christ. They supposedly stuck nails into the wafers or cut them with knives until blood flowed, which would have been evidence to support the teachings of transsubstantiation."

Christine Mittlmeier
Literaturhistorikerin
\ Literary Historian

3
Hostienfrevel vor dem Schwabinger Tor
München, 1624
Öl auf Fichtenholz
H: 156 cm, B: 212 cm

Diözesanmuseum Freising, # M.566
Dauerleihgabe des Metropolitankapitels München

>>

3
The Desecration of the Host outside Schwabing Gate
Munich, 1624
Oil on panel (spruce)
H: 156 cm, W: 212 cm

Diözesanmuseum Freising, # M.566
On permanent loan from the Metropolitan Chapter of Munich

>>

Umwandlung der Synagoge in eine Kirche 1442

Nachdem es in München bereits 1285 und 1349 zu Pogromen und vorübergehenden Vertreibungen gekommen war, wurden die Juden 1442 unter Herzog Albrecht III. dauerhaft vertrieben. Bis in das 18. Jahrhundert war ihnen nun der Aufenthalt in München und dem gesamten Herzogtum Bayern verboten.

Die Synagoge der 1442 vertriebenen Gemeinde, die sich auf dem Gelände des heutigen Marienhofs befand, schenkte der Herzog seinem Leibarzt Johann Hartlieb, der im Kellergewölbe, der „Gruft", eine Marienkapelle einrichten ließ. Wenige Jahre später wurde auch das Erdgeschoss – möglicherweise der ehemalige Betraum der Synagoge – in eine Kirche umgewandelt. Die in der Gruftkirche zur Aufstellung gelangte Pietà – eine Darstellung Marias als Schmerzensmutter mit dem Leichnam Jesu in ihren Armen – wurde bald zu einem bedeutenden Anziehungspunkt für Wallfahrer. Noch im 19. Jahrhundert wurde die Legende verbreitet, dass diese Pietà nach 1442 unter dem Fußboden, wo sie Juden vor der Vertreibung verscharrt hätten, aufgefunden worden sei.

Theologischer Hintergrund für die Umwandlung von Synagogen in Marienkirchen war zum einen eine Demonstration der angeblichen Schuld der Juden am Tod Jesu, die durch den geschundenen Leichnam und die Schmerzensmutter eindringlich visualisiert wurde. Zum anderen handelte es sich um ein Reinigungsritual, durch das der aus christlicher Sicht unreine Ort der Synagoge durch Maria, dem christlichen Symbol der Unbefleckheit, in einen reinen Ort transformiert wurde. Die Erinnerung daran, dass die Gruftkirche einst Synagoge war, blieb lange wach. 1753 entdeckten Bauarbeiter bei einem Umbau der Gruftkirche Knochen und ein angeblich in einer vermauerten Nische brennendes Öllicht. Zeitgenossen brachten diesen Fund mit angeblichen Ritualmorden des Mittelalters in Verbindung.

1803 wurde die Gruftkirche im Zuge der Säkularisierung geschlossen und später abgebrochen. Die Pietà, die 350 Jahre in der ehemaligen Synagoge verehrt wurde, gelangte im Laufe des 19. Jahrhunderts in die Kirche von Salmdorf bei Haar und zählt heute zu den bedeutendsten Beispielen spätmittelalterlicher Vesperbilder Europas.

[B.Pu.]

Conversion of Synagogue to a Church in 1442

After the pogroms of 1285 and 1349 and temporary expulsion from Munich, the Jews were exiled permanently in 1442 under Duke Albrecht III. Their residence in Munich or the Duchy of Bavaria as a whole was forbidden right up until the 18th century.

The synagogue used by the community until its expulsion in 1442, located on the site of what is today the Marienhof, was given by the Duke to his personal physician Johann Hartlieb, who had a chapel dedicated to the Virgin Mary built in the vaulted crypt. A few years later, the ground floor—possibly the former prayer room in the synagogue—was converted into a church. The *Pietà* displayed in the chapel in the crypt, depicting the Virgin Mary cradling the body of her son in her arms, soon became an important point of pilgrimage. Even in the 19th century, the legend was still widespread that this *Pietà*, found under the floor after 1442, had been buried by the Jews before their expulsion.

The theological thinking behind this was, on the one hand, to demonstrate the alleged guilt of the Jews for the death of Christ, strikingly rendered by the body with its visible wounds and the mourning Virgin, and on the other hand, to transform the synagogue, which—from a Christian point of view—was seen as an impure place, into a place of purity through the Virgin Mary, the Christian symbol of the immaculate state. However, the memory of the crypt chapel as a former synagogue was upheld for a long time. In 1753, builders carrying out construction work in the chapel came across bones and an oil lamp in a walled-up niche that was reputedly still burning. Contemporary witnesses linked these finds with ritual murders that were allegedly committed in the Middle Ages.

In 1803, the church was closed during secularisation and later demolished. The *Pietà*, that had been worshiped for 350 years in the former synagogue, found its way to the church in Salmdorf near Haar in the course of the 19th century and is now regarded as one of the most important *Pietà* of the Late Middle Ages in Europe.

„Dieser Kult dauerte bis in die Reformationszeit und geriet dann fast in Vergessenheit. Aber zu Beginn des 17. Jahrhunderts ist er durch eine Traumvision wieder aufgelebt und hat bis zur Säkularisation geblüht. Dass in der Kirche im Gruftgässlein gerade Maria besonders verehrt wurde, kommt nicht von ungefähr, denn Maria ist in der christlichen Kirche die Allegorie der Kirche. Sie ist an verschiedenen Orten in Süddeutschland auf einstigen Synagogen, in darüber gebauten Marien-Gnadenkirchen zu finden, so in Würzburg, in Nürnberg, in Regensburg und andernorts."

"This cult lasted until the Reformation and was then almost lost in oblivion. However, at the beginning of the 17th century, following the vision someone had in a dream, it enjoyed a revival which continued until the Secularisation. That the crypt chapel in the little alley was dedicated to the Virgin Mary was not a coincidence, as the symbolic status of the Virgin Mary in the Christian church is of particular importance. Churches dedicated to the Virgin Mary can be found on the sites of many former synagogues, as in Würzburg, Nuremberg, Bamberg, and Regensburg."

Wolfgang Brückner
Volkskundler
\ European Ethnologist

**4
Pietà von Salmdorf**
München (?), um 1340
Pappelholz mit Resten
verschiedener polychromer
Fassungen
H: 183 cm

Filialkirchenstiftung
Maria Himmelfahrt
Salmdorf in der Pfarrei Ottendichl,
Gemeinde Haar

**4
The Salmdorf Pietà**
Munich (?), c. 1340
Panel (poplar) with traces
of various polychromatic
reworkings
H: 183 cm

Ottendichl Parish –
Filialkirchenstiftung Salmdorf

Judenpolitik Herzog Albrechts V. im 16. Jahrhundert

Seit der von Herzog Albrecht III. angeordneten Vertreibung der Juden im Jahr 1442 war für diese ein Leben in der Residenzstadt wie im Herzogtum Bayern nahezu unmöglich. So war Juden nicht nur das Hausieren und das Betreiben eines Gewerbes, sondern auch die Ansiedlung innerhalb der Grenzen Bayerns untersagt.

Im Jahr 1553 bestätigte die Landesordnung von Herzog Albrecht V. das Verbot. Standen die Vertreibungen des Spätmittelalters und der Frühen Neuzeit mit den Vorwürfen des Ritualmordes, der Hostienschändung und des wucherischen Handels in Verbindung, so hatte Albrecht V. andere Beweggründe. Da sich bereits seit 1442 keine Juden mehr im Herzogtum Bayern aufhalten durften, konnte eine angebliche wirtschaftliche Beeinträchtigung der christlichen Bevölkerung durch die Juden für die Erneuerung des Aufenthaltsverbotes nicht ausschlaggebend gewesen sein. Vielmehr ist die Landesordnung als Werkzeug Albrechts V. zu verstehen, dessen er sich bediente, um die Vorherrschaft des Katholizismus in Bayern zu unterstreichen. Im Interesse der Sicherung seiner Herrschaft versuchte er gleichzeitig, die protestantischen Landstände Bayerns, die politisch in Opposition zu ihm standen, für sich zu gewinnen. Im christlich fundierten Antijudaismus stimmten Protestanten und Katholiken nämlich überein, und mit der Bestätigung des Ansiedlungsverbots kam Albrecht V. deren gemeinsamer Forderung nach.

Die Politik Albrechts V. war von religiöser Intoleranz gekennzeichnet. Im Zuge des Aufbaus seiner, für die Renaissance typischen Kunst- und Wunderkammer wurde Albrecht V. als Sammler von jüdischen Handschriften und Ritualobjekten allerdings ungewollt zu einem Bewahrer mittelalterlicher und frühneuzeitlicher Zeugnisse jener Minderheit, die er des Landes verwiesen hatte.

Der Ausschluss der Juden aus München und Bayern wurde von den Nachfolgern Albrechts V. bestätigt. Erst die aufwändige Hofhaltung und der damit verbundene Geldbedarf machten es im frühen 18. Jahrhundert für einzelne Juden möglich, als Finanziers des Hofes in München zu leben.

[T.Ne.]

The Jewish Policy of Duke Albrecht V in the 16th Century

Following the expulsion of the Jews in 1442 by Duke Albrecht III, it was virtually impossible for a Jew to live either in the Bavarian capital or in the Duchy at all. Jews were not just prohibited from selling their wares and running a business, but also from settling anywhere within the Bavarian borders.

In 1553 this prohibition was reconfirmed by Duke Albrecht V. While persecution in the Late Middle Ages and the early modern era was associated with accusations of ritual murder, the desecration of the Host, and exorbitant trading practices, Albrecht V had different reasons for his actions. Since no Jews were permitted to live in the Duchy of Bavaria from 1442 onward, no alleged economic curtailment of the Christian population by the Jews could possibly have been crucial to the renewal of the prohibition. Albrecht V's directive should be seen much more as underlining the dominance of Catholicism in Bavaria. In the interests of securing his position, he also attempted to gain the favor of the Protestant estates in Bavaria, who were his political opponents at the same time. Protestants and Catholics both adopted the same anti-Jewish stance anchored in the Christian church, and by confirming the settlement prohibition Albrecht V was fulfilling their common wish.

Albrecht V's policies were characterised by their religious intolerance. In the course of building up his Cabinet of Art and Curiosities—so typical of the Renaissance period—Albrecht V unwittingly became the keeper of objects from the Middle Ages and early modern era that bore testimony to the minority group itself that he had expelled from his country, as his collection included Jewish manuscripts and ritual objects.

The exclusion of Jews from Munich and Bavaria was propagated by Albrecht V's descendants. Only the extravagances of keeping court and the associated financial necessities rendered it possible for individual Jews to live at court in Munich as financiers in the early 18th century.

„Mit seiner antijüdischen Gesetzgebung erfüllte Albrecht V. auch eine Forderung der bayerischen Landstände: Ungeachtet der konfessionellen Gegensätze - Albrecht V. galt als gutkatholisch, die Landstände sympathisierten teilweise mit dem Protestantismus - war man sich im christlich fundierten Antijudaismus einig. Albrecht sah auch keinen Widerspruch zwischen seiner religiösen Intoleranz und seiner bedeutenden Sammlung hebräischer Literatur und jüdischer Kultgeräte. Er war weder besonders kunstsinnig noch speziell an jüdischer Kultur interessiert. Sein Interesse galt vor allem der Steigerung seiner fürstlichen Reputation."

"Through his anti-Jewish laws, Albrecht V also met the demands of the Bavarian estates: Irrespective of religious differences—Albrecht V was regarded as a devout Catholic while the estates had certain Protestant sympathies—both adopted the same anti-Jewish stance anchored in the Christian church. Albrecht did not see any contradiction between his religious intolerance and his important collection of Hebrew literature and Jewish ritual objects. He had neither a particular artistic bent nor did he have a special interest in Jewish culture. His focus was purely on increasing his princely reputation."

Dietmar Heil
Historiker \ Historian

5
Herzog Albrecht V.
Umkreis von Ignaz Günther
München, um 1770/1777
Lindenholz
H: 62,5 cm

Bayerisches Nationalmuseum, R 1740

5
Duke Albrecht V
Circle of Ignaz Günther
Munich, c. 1770/1777
Panel (limewood)
H: 62.5 cm

Bayerisches Nationalmuseum, R 1740

Ahasver, der Ewige Jude in München

Die Legende von Ahasver, dem Ewigen Juden, ist seit dem Mittelalter bekannt und wurde seit dem frühen 17. Jahrhundert durch Flugschriften populär. Sie erzählt von einem Schuster, der Jesus auf dem Kreuzweg von seiner Treppe wies, deshalb zu ewiger Wanderschaft verdammt wurde und seither rastlos durch die Welt irrt.

Zahlreiche Sagenbücher datieren einen der Besuche des Ewigen Juden in München auf das Jahr 1721, als ihm der Einlass am Isartor verweigert worden sein soll und er sich mehrere Wochen bei der Kirche St. Nikola am Gasteig aufgehalten haben soll. Im 19. Jahrhundert erschienen mehrere Romane und Erzählungen, die sich dem Aufenthalt Ahasvers in München widmeten, und 1910 erzählt der Schriftsteller Guillaume Apollinaire von einer Begegnung mit dem Ewigen Juden in Prag, bei der dieser auch zwei Besuche in München, 1334 und 1721, erwähnt. Kurz nach dem Ersten Weltkrieg greift Lion Feuchtwanger das Motiv auf und lässt seine Erzählung „Gespräche mit dem Ewigen Juden" mit den Worten beginnen: „Vor einem Jahr etwa traf ich den Ewigen Juden in München. Er saß im Café Odeon und las die ‚Frankfurter Zeitung'".

Während antijüdische Stereotypen in den frühen Erzählungen über den Ewigen Juden nicht im Mittelpunkt der Darstellung stehen, wird das von ihm gezeichnete Bild im 19. Jahrhundert zunehmend antisemitischer. Der Münchner Maler Wilhelm von Kaulbach stellt in seinem 1843 von König Ludwig I. in Auftrag gegebenen Monumentalgemälde „Die Zerstörung Jerusalems" (Neue Pinakothek) Ahasver als Symbol der Niederlage des Judentums und als Antithese zur christlichen Familie dar. In München tätige jüdische Künstler wie Maurycy Gottlieb oder Samuel Hirszenberg reagierten später in ihren Werken auf die antisemitische Darstellung Kaulbachs und entwarfen ein positives Gegenbild des Ewigen Juden, das die Diaspora-Erfahrung mit einschloss.

Während der NS-Zeit wurde der Ewige Jude schließlich zur Verkörperung alles Verwerflichen, das Juden unterstellt wurde. Das Plakat der 1937 im Deutschen Museum gezeigten Hetzausstellung „Der ewige Jude" zeichnet das Bild einer hässlichen Person, die in ihren Attributen Weltherrschaftsphantasien, Kapitalismus und Kommunismus vereint. Die Münchner Ausstellung und ein unter gleichem Titel im Jahr 1940 produzierter „Dokumentarfilm" trugen maßgeblich dazu bei, jene Stimmung in der deutschen Bevölkerung aufzubauen und zu verstärken, die den Holocaust ermöglichte.

[B.Pu.]

Ahasver, the Wandering Jew in Munich

The legend of Ahasver, the Wandering Jew, has been passed down since the Middle Ages and became popular in the early 17th century through booklets. It relates the tale of a shoemaker who turned Jesus away from his steps on the way to the Crucifixion and was then cursed to walk the earth for all eternity.

Numerous books of legends date a visit to Munich by the Wandering Jew to 1721, when he was not allowed to pass the Isar Gate and who then reputedly stayed several weeks near St Nicholas's Church in the area of the Gasteig. In the 19th century, several novels and short stories were published on Ahasver's stay in Munich, and in 1910 the French writer Guillaume Apollinaire told of his meeting the Wandering Jew in Prague, and also mentions two visits to Munich—in 1334 and 1721. Shortly after the First World War, Lion Feuchtwanger picked on this motif and began his short story *Conversations with the Wandering Jew* with the lines: "A year ago I met the Wandering Jew in Munich. He was sitting in the Odeon Café reading the 'Frankfurter Zeitung'."

While anti-Jewish stereotypes did not dominate the character in early tales of the Wandering Jew, his depiction became increasingly anti-Semitic from the 19th century onward. In his monumental painting *The Destruction of Jerusalem* (Neue Pinakothek), commissioned by King Ludwig I in 1843, the artist Wilhelm von Kaulbach of Munich depicted Ahasver as the symbol of the decline of Judaism and as the antithesis of the Christian family. Jewish artists working in Munich, such as Maurycy Gottlieb and Samuel Hirszenberg, later showed their reaction to Kaulbach's anti-Semitic depiction in their own works by creating a counterpoint to the Wandering Jew, which incorporated the experience of the diaspora.

During the period under the National Socialists, the Wandering Jew became the embodiment of everything condemnable that was attributed to the Jews. The poster for the exhibition "Der ewige Jude" (The Wandering—or lit. Eternal—Jew), held in the Deutsches Museum in 1937, aimed to propagate hatred, and depicts an ugly person, who embodies dreams of world supremacy, capitalism, and communism in one. The Munich exhibition and a "documentary" film produced in 1940 with the same title, played a major role in creating and strengthening a feeling among the German populace that made the Holocaust possible in the first place.

„Die Ausgestaltung der Legende bildet sich im 17. Jahrhundert umfassend heraus, und von diesem Zeitpunkt an können wir sehen, wie sich die Sage in viele verschiedene Länder ausbreitet und in schriftlichen und bildlichen Zeugnissen an verschiedenen Orten auftaucht. Christen wollten dem Ewigen Juden begegnen, weil er in authentischer Weise das Ereignis der Passion Christi miterlebt hat. Gegen Ende des 19. Jahrhunderts beschäftigten sich jüdische Künstler mit dieser christologischen Legende. Sie sehen darin sehr deutliche jüdische Aspekte, weil der Ewige Jude in einem gewissen Sinn die eigenen Erfahrungen der Juden durch die Jahrhunderte zum Ausdruck bringt."

"The form of the legend emerges full-blown in the 17th century and from then on we can beginn to see that the Wandering Jew spreads himself in many different countries, appears in many different places in texts and visual material and Christian individuals want to encounter the Wandering Jew because he has the secret of the original moment in which Christ was at the passion. At some point towards the end of the 19th century there are Jewish artists who begin to think that this Christological legend really has a very clear Jewish aspect because the Wandering Jew in a sense expresses the internal experience of Jews over time."

Richard I. Cohen
Historiker \ Historian

**6
Kleiderständer mit Regenschirm und „Frankfurter Zeitung"**
Deutschland, um 1880/1900
Eisen, teilweise lackiert
H: 190 cm

Jüdisches Museum München,
JM 7/2008, JM 8/2008, JM 6/2008

**6
Clothes Stand with Umbrella and the "Frankfurter Zeitung"**
Germany, c. 1880/1900
Iron, painted in parts
H: 190 cm

Jewish Museum Munich,
JM 7/2008, JM 8/2008, JM 6/2008

Juden als geduldete Geldgeber im 18. Jahrhundert

Erstmals seit über 250 Jahren konnten sich Anfang des 18. Jahrhunderts einzelne Juden wieder innerhalb der Stadtmauern Münchens aufhalten. Als Finanziers des Spanischen Erbfolgekriegs waren sie jedoch nur vorübergehend willkommen. 1715 ließ Max Emanuel II. erneut alle Juden aus dem Kurfürstentum Bayern ausweisen.

Der luxuriöse Lebensstil am Münchner Hof und der damit verbundene Finanzbedarf machten es aber wenige Jahre später wieder notwendig, jüdische Bankiers in die Stadt zu lassen, da diese im Gegensatz zu christlichen Finanziers bereit waren, den völlig überschuldeten Hof mit Krediten zu bedienen. Zu den sich in der Stadt niederlassenden Juden zählten auch Angehörige der weit verzweigten Familie Wertheimer. Wolf Simon Wertheimer und sein Sohn Samuel Wolf ließen sich „Im Tal" nahe dem Alten Rathaus nieder, richteten dort die erste, kleine Synagoge nach der Vertreibung von 1442 ein und zählten zu den wichtigsten Geldgebern der Wittelsbacher.

Als der Staat allerdings seiner Schuldentilgung immer schleppender nachkam, brachte dies die Münchner Wertheimer zunehmend in Bedrängnis und führte dazu, dass ihre Bedeutung und ihr Einfluss innerhalb des Kreises der süddeutschen Hofjuden immer mehr verblasste.

1779 stellte Kurfürst Karl Theodor diesen „Freypass-Brief" für Josef Samuel Wertheimer, dem Enkel Wolf Simon Wertheimers, aus. Die darin zugesicherten, umfangreichen Privilegien und Hilfestellungen bei Reisen dienten wohl als Beruhigung und „Trostpflaster" für den Träger, der sich, wie schon sein Vater und sein Großvater, erfolglos darum bemüht hatte, die längst fälligen Kreditschulden einzufordern. Zwar unternahm der Staat 1768 einen Versuch, die Schuldenrückzahlung wieder aufzunehmen, stellte aber 1784 nach Begleichung einiger Rückstände, die auf Druck des österreichischen Kaisers Josef II. geleistet wurden, die Rückzahlungen völlig ein.

Josef Samuel Wertheimer übersiedelte nach Wien, wo er 1791 von Kaiser Leopold II. als Eduard von Wertheimstein in den Adelsstand erhoben wurde und 1811 verstarb.

[B.Pu.]

Jews as Tolerated Moneylenders in the 18th Century

At the beginning of the 18th century, certain Jews were allowed to live inside the city walls for the first time in more than 250 years. As financiers in the War of the Spanish Succession they were however only temporarily welcome. By 1715, Max Emanuel II had all Jews expelled once again from the Electorate of Bavaria.

The luxurious lifestyle at the Court of Munich and its associated financial outlay made it necessary to let Jewish bankers back into the city just a few years later, as unlike Christian financiers, the Jews were prepared to grant loans to the utterly destitute Court. Among those who moved to the city were members of the widespread Wertheimer family. Wolf Simon Wertheimer and his son Samuel Wolf settled in the street "Im Tal," not far from the old City Hall, opened the first small synagogue after the expulsion of the Jews in 1442, and were among the Wittelsbachers' most important money-lenders.

When the city became increasingly bad at paying off its debts, the Wertheimers found themselves in an extremely difficult situation, to such an extent that their influence within the circle of Court Jews in southern German became less and less.

In 1779, the Elector Karl Theodor presented Josef Samuel Wertheimer—Simon Wertheimer's grandson—with the "Free Charter." The considerable privileges and assistance on journeys accorded to him were intended more to placate and be a form of consolation to the charter holder, who like his father and grandfather before him, had tried unsuccessfully to collect the debts on long overdue loans. Although the city attempted to resume paying back its debts in 1768, it stopped redemptions completely in 1784 after settling several outstanding payments as a result of pressure exerted by the Austrian Emperor Josef II.

Josef Samuel Wertheimer moved to Vienna and was raised to the nobility in 1791 by Emperor Leopold II, where he was known as Eduard von Wertheimstein. He died in 1811.

Rolf Kießling
Historiker \ Historian

„Da seit dem Verbot der Ansiedlung und des Handels den Juden in Bayern im 15. und 16. Jahrhundert das Wohnrecht in München nicht gestattet ist, muss über die Privilegierung des Kurfürsten die Möglichkeit des Agierens in München erst geschaffen werden. Das geschieht zunächst einmal für die Familien, die sich um die Wertheimers gruppieren und „Im Tal" in den Weinwirtschaften Logis nehmen, wobei sich die Wohnung der Wertheimers zu einer Art Zentrum herauskristallisiert."

"Since the prohibition order against Jews settling and trading in Bavaria in the 15th and 16th centuries also forebade them from living in Munich, the possibility for carrying on a business in Munich first had to be established through a privilege granted by the Elector. This happened first of all to those families connected to the Wertheimers and those who had taken up lodgings in the wine taverns in the street 'Im Tal'—with the Wertheimers' apartment becoming a sort of focal point."

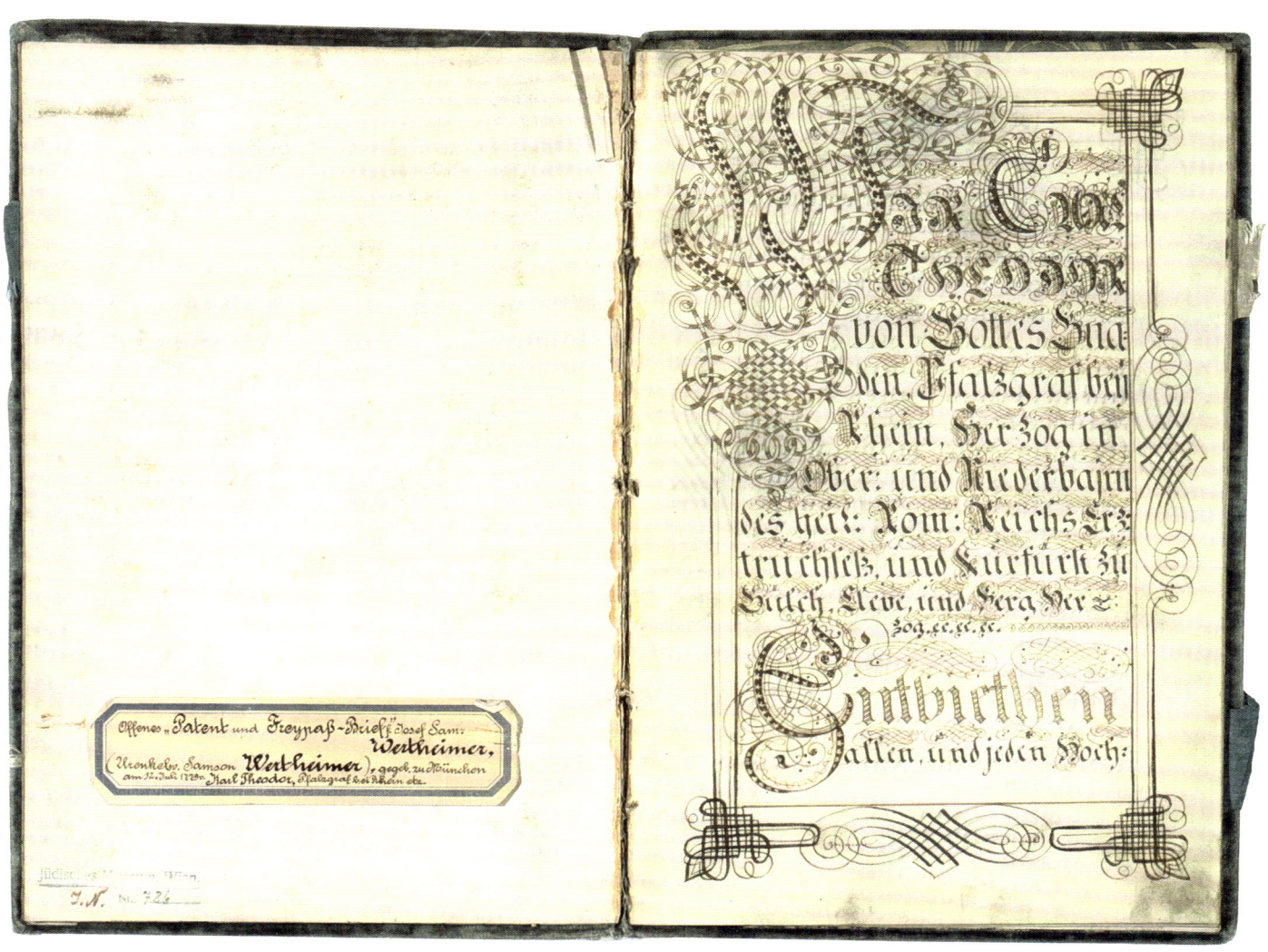

7
**Offenes Patent und Freypass-Brief
für Josef Samuel Wertheimer**
München, 12. Juli 1779
Tinte auf Pergament, Samteinband
4°

Jüdisches Museum der Stadt Wien, # 4061

7
**Unrestricted Letters Patent and "Free Charter"
given to Josef Samuel Wertheimer**
Munich, July 12, 1779
Ink on parchment with velvet binding
4°

Jewish Museum Vienna, # 4061

Taufe als Entre Billet in die Gesellschaft um 1800

Am achten Tag nach der Geburt wird ein jüdischer Knabe beschnitten und findet damit Aufnahme in den Bund Abrahams. Die Stoffwindel, die zur Wundabdeckung verwendet wird, wurde in den deutschsprachigen aschkenasischen Gemeinden ab dem 16. Jahrhundert als Beschneidungs- oder Tora-Wimpel (hebr. Mappa) zum Kultgegenstand. Der Wimpel wurde kunstvoll mit dem hebräischen Namen des Kindes, dem Vaternamen und dem Geburtsdatum sowie einem Segensspruch bestickt bzw. bemalt. Zwischen dem ersten und dritten Lebensjahr überbrachte ihn der Knabe der Synagoge, wo er zum Umwickeln der Tora-Rollen verwendet wurde. Der Tora-Wimpel ist gleichzeitig Zeugnis jüdischen Brauchtums und kultureller Transfers: Neben jüdischer Symbolik enthält er auch volkstümliche Elemente, die ihn zu einer einzigartigen Quelle machen.

Als Naftali, genannt Hirz, Ulmann sich im Jahr 1812 mit 40 Jahren zur Taufe entschied und in der Kirche St. Moritz in Augsburg den katholischen Glauben annahm und sich fortan Moritz Mayer nannte, hatte für ihn der Tora-Wimpel seine Bedeutung als Beleg für den Bund Abrahams verloren. Trotzdem dauerte es weitere 24 Jahre, bis er ihn aus den Händen gab, allerdings nicht ohne eine ausführliche schriftliche Erklärung über Herkunft, Gebrauch und Inhalt des Wimpels beizufügen. Vielleicht hat er den Wimpel dem Herrscherhaus geschenkt, wie dies nicht unüblich war. Aus der alten und ruhmreichen jüdischen Familie Ulmann-Günzburg stammend, deren Ahnentafel bis in das 16. Jahrhundert zurückreicht, hatte er vielleicht wie viele andere gehofft, die Taufe möge seine Eintrittskarte in die bürgerliche Gesellschaft sein.

Da Juden vor der bürgerlichen Gleichstellung, die in Bayern 1871 erfolgte, nicht die gleichen Rechte wie die christlichen Bürger hatten, war die Taufe, der Übertritt zum Christentum, die einzige Möglichkeit, das volle Bürgerrecht zu erhalten.

Diese Hoffnung erfüllte sich für Moritz Mayer nur teilweise: Zwar erhielt der Konvertit 1823 eine Anstellung als Verwaltungsbeamter bei der königlichen Schuldentilgungskommission, aber schon fünf Jahre später wurde er wegen einer Augenkrankheit als Mittelloser in das St. Josephs-Spital in München aufgenommen. Seine Spitalskosten zahlte eine katholische Stiftung. Seine beiden ebenfalls getauften Kinder Karl und Wilhelmine erhielten kein Aufenthaltsrecht in München und wohnten in Pfersee bzw. Fellheim.

[B.St.]

Baptism as Entry Ticket to Society, c. 1800

On the eighth day after birth, a Jewish boy is circumcised and is accepted into the Covenant of Abraham. The cloth used to dress the wound, became a ritual object in German-speaking Ashkenazi communities from the 16th century onward, and was known as a circumcision or Torah binder (Hebrew: *mappa*). The binder would be artistically embroidered or painted with the Hebrew name of the child, the father's name, the date of birth, and a blessing. Between the age of one and three, the young boy would present it to the synagogue to be wrapped around the Torah scrolls. This particular Torah binder is both a testimony to Jewish tradition and to a cultural change: In addition to its Jewish symbolism, it also bears other popular elements that make it a unique source of information.

When Naftali, known as Hirz, Ulmann decided to be baptised in St. Moritz' Church in Augsburg in 1812 at the age of forty, and to convert to the Catholic faith, after which time he was called Moritz Mayer, the Torah binder had, for him, lost its meaning as a symbol of the Covenant of Abraham. However it would take another 24 years before he gave it away, and even then not without a detailed written explanation of its origin, use, and the inscriptions on the binder. It may be that he presented the binder to the ruling house—something that was not unusual at that time. Descended from the old, highly-respected Jewish family, the Ulmann-Günzburgs, whose ancestry can be traced back to the 16th century, he may have hoped, like many others, that his baptism would enable him to enjoy common civic privileges.

Before equal rights were granted in Bavaria in 1871, Jews did not enjoy the same privileges as Christians. Baptism and conversion to the Catholic Church was for many the only possibility of benefitting from standard civil rights.

This wish only came partially true for Moritz Mayer: Although the convert was appointed to the position of clerk in the Royal Debts Commission, five years later he was admitted to St. Joseph's Hospice in Munich as a pauper due to an eye illness. Hospice expenses were paid by the Catholic church. Neither of his two children, Karl and Wilhelmine, where granted the right of abode in Munich and lived in Pfersee and Fellheim, respectively.

„Nun waren es Juden selbst, die in einer Zeit schleppender bürgerlicher Gleichstellung in der Taufe die Chance auf eine Beschleunigung sahen. Das Entre Billet, die Eintrittskarte in die bürgerliche Gesellschaft, wie der Dichter Heinrich Heine den Übertritt zum Christentum bezeichnete, hat sich jedoch als Täuschung herausgestellt: Mit dem Entstehen des rassistischen Antisemitismus, der im 20. Jahrhundert in die Nürnberger Rassengesetze und letztendlich in den Holocaust mündete, war auch die Taufe, der Übertritt zum Christentum, für Juden keine Versicherung mehr gegen Verfolgung und Vernichtung."

"It was now the Jews themselves who, at a time when equal civil rights were slow in coming, saw baptism as a way to speed things up. The 'entre billet,' the entrance ticket to civil society, as the poet Heinrich Heine described this conversion to Christianity, turned out to be a deception. With the emergence of racist anti-Semitism that led to the discriminatory Nuremberg Laws in the 20th century and ultimately to the Holocaust, baptism—the conversion to Christianity—no longer gave Jews any protection against persecution and annihilation."

Bernhard Purin
Kulturwissenschaftler
\ Cultural Studies Scholar

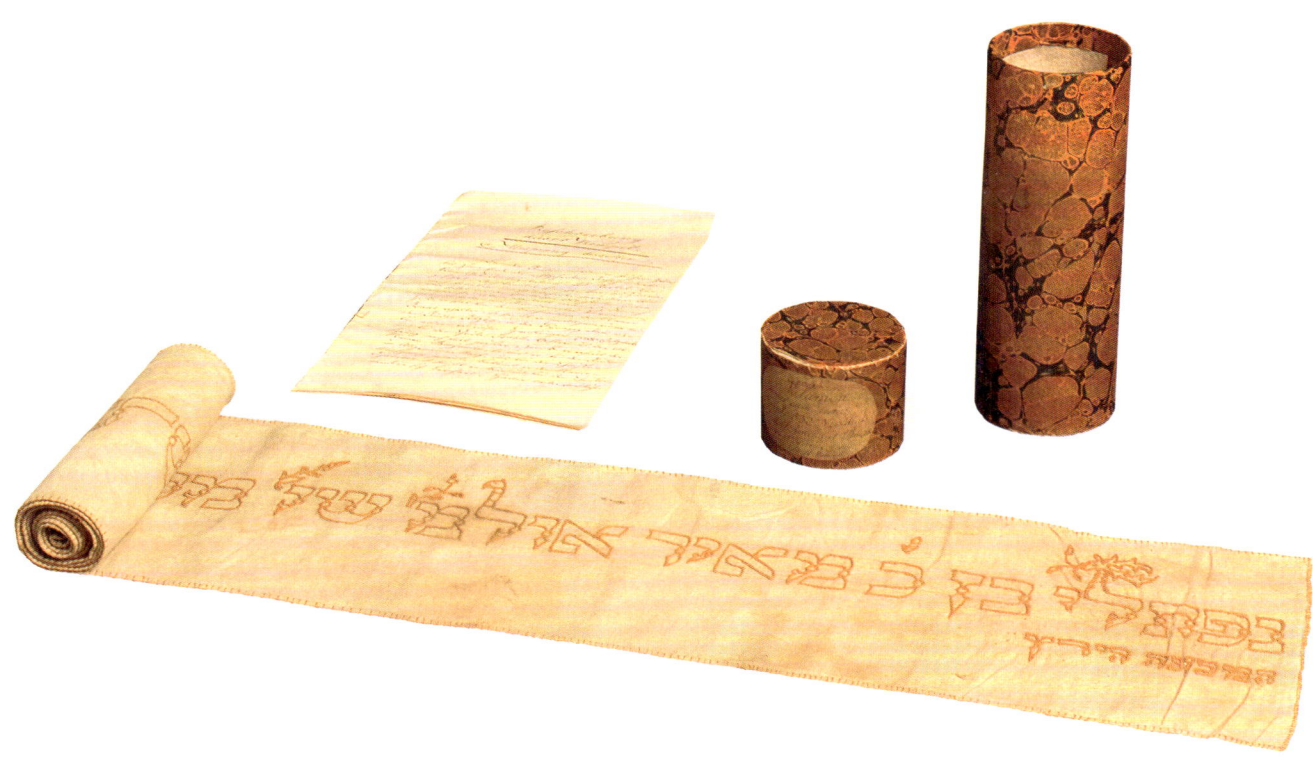

8
**Tora-Wimpel des Konvertiten
Naftali Hirz b. Me'ir Ulmann**
Augsburg-Pfersee, 1772
Leinen, gestickt
L: 286 cm, H: 20,5 cm

Bayerische Staatsbibliothek, München, Sign. Cod. Hebr. 498(3

Inschrift: Naftali genannt Hirz Sohn des Herrn Me'ir Ulmann, er soll leben, aus Pfersee, geboren am Sonntag, den 17. Kislev 532 nach der kleinen Zählung [27. November 1772]. Er wachse heran zur Tora, zur Chuppa und zu Guten Werken. Amen Sela.

8
**Torah Binder owned by the Convert
Naftali Hirz b. Me'ir Ulmann**
Augsburg-Pfersee, 1772
Linen, embroidered
L: 286 cm, H: 20.5 cm

Bayerische Staatsbibliothek, Munich, Sign. Cod. Hebr. 498(3

Inscription: Naftali known as Hirz, son of Me'ir Ulmann, long may he live, of Pfersee, born on Sunday, on the 17th day of the month of Kislev, 532, according to the Jewish calendar [27 November, 1772]. May he grow to the Torah, the Chuppah, and to good deeds. Amen Sela.

Katholischer Antisemitismus um 1900

Im ausgehenden 19. Jahrhundert entwickelte sich aus dem traditionellen Antijudaismus der moderne Antisemitismus. Während die Feindschaft gegen die Juden in den vorangegangenen Jahrhunderten vornehmlich religiös begründet worden war, entwickelte sich der Diskurs nun zunehmend in eine rassistische und nationalistische Richtung.

Georg Ratzinger, Priester, Abgeordneter und Vertreter der katholischen Soziallehre, lebte seit 1868 in München. Unter dem Pseudonym Dr. Robert Waldhausen veröffentlichte er 1893 dieses Pamphlet, in welchem er die Juden für sämtliche soziale Missstände in der Gesellschaft verantwortlich machte. Er bezeichnete sie als Wucherer, die ihre Umwelt zugunsten ihres eigenen Wohlstands gewissenlos ausbeuteten. Als Konsequenz forderte Ratzinger eine Kennzeichnung der Juden und ihren Ausschluss aus dem gesellschaftlichen Leben. Auch eine Tätigkeit im öffentlichen Dienst sollte ihnen verwehrt werden. In seinem späteren Werk „Das Judentum in Bayern", das er unter dem Pseudonym Dr. Gottfried Wolf veröffentlichte, verschärfte er seine antisemitische Polemik. Er bezichtigte die Juden, denen er einen grundsätzlichen Mangel an sittlichem Bewusstsein bescheinigte, nun auch der Vorbereitung einer Weltverschwörung.

Im Antisemitismus sah Ratzinger eine gleichermaßen sittlich wie ökonomisch begründete Form der Abwehr dieser Gefahren durch die christliche Bevölkerung. Als Mitglied des Bayerischen Landtags war er mehrfach mit Klagen des „Vereins zur Abwehr des Antisemitismus" konfrontiert.

Seit einigen Jahren erfährt das Werk Georg Ratzingers, dessen Bedeutung als Vertreter der katholischen Soziallehre hervorgehoben wird, in Teilen der katholischen Kirche eine Renaissance. Das wieder belebte Interesse an Ratzingers Person lässt sich auch auf die verwandtschaftliche Nähe zu Benedikt XVI. – Ratzinger war ein Großonkel des Papstes – zurückführen.

Sein antisemitischer Grundtenor wird – wie bei der Neuausgabe seines Hauptwerks über die kirchliche Armenpflege – als „zeitgebundene Haltung" verharmlost oder gänzlich ausgeblendet.

[T.Ne.]

Catholic Anti-Semitism, c. 1900

At the end of the 19th century, long-standing anti-Jewish sentiments developed into modern-day anti-Semitism. While the animosity shown toward Jews over past centuries was generally of a religious nature, the discourse at this time evolved more and more in a racist and nationalistic direction.

Georg Ratzinger, priest, Member of Parliament, and advocate of Catholic social teaching, had been living in Munich since 1868. Under the pseudonym Dr. Robert Waldhausen he published this pamphlet in 1893, in which he blamed the Jews for all social problems of that time. He called them profiteers, who unscrupulously took advantage of everything about them to further their own standing. As a consequence, Ratzinger demanded a form of identification for Jews and that they be excluded from common societal life. They should also be prohibited from working in the public sector. In his later work, *Judaism in Bavaria*, that he published under the pseudonym Dr. Gottfried Wolf, he sharpened the tone of his anti-Semitic polemic. He accused the Jews, who he considered as basically lacking any moral awareness, of planning a conspiracy of global proportions.

Ratzinger considered anti-Semitism both an ethically and economically justified form of defence against dangers faced by the Christian population. As a member of the Bavarian parliament, he had—on many occasions—to deal with complaints from the "Association for the Defence against Anti-Semitism."

For several years now, the work of Georg Ratzinger, whose importance as an advocate of Catholic social teaching has always been particularly emphasised, has experienced a renaissance in certain sectors of the Catholic church. This renewed interest in Ratzinger as a person can certainly be atrributed to his family ties to Benedict XVI—Georg Ratzinger was the present Pope's great uncle.

His anti-Semitic stance is played down as being an "attitude common at that time" or is even completely omitted, as in the new edition of his major work on Christian aid for the poor.

„Überhaupt ist zu dieser Zeit der Antisemitismus zu so etwas wie zu einem politischen Totalprogramm auch auf der katholischen Seite geworden. Da die Juden nun an allem schuld waren, was die Moderne zu bieten hatte – Liberalismus, Sozialdemokratie, überhaupt der Kapitalismus –, wurde gleichsam in einem Elften Gebot, nämlich „Du sollst Antisemit sein", auch der Antisemitismus zum Konzentrat wirklichen christlichen Glaubens, und das war eine verhängnisvolle Entwicklung."

'During this period as a whole, anti-Semitism evolved into something akin to an entire political agenda on the Catholic side as well. As Jews were now responsible for everything that the modern era had to offer– liberalism, social democracy, even capitalism in general– anti-Semitism became a core issue of true Christian belief in the form of an Eleventh Commandment: 'Thou shalt be anti-Semitic'–a development that would prove disastrous."

Kurt Greussing
Politikwissenschaftler
\ Political Scientist

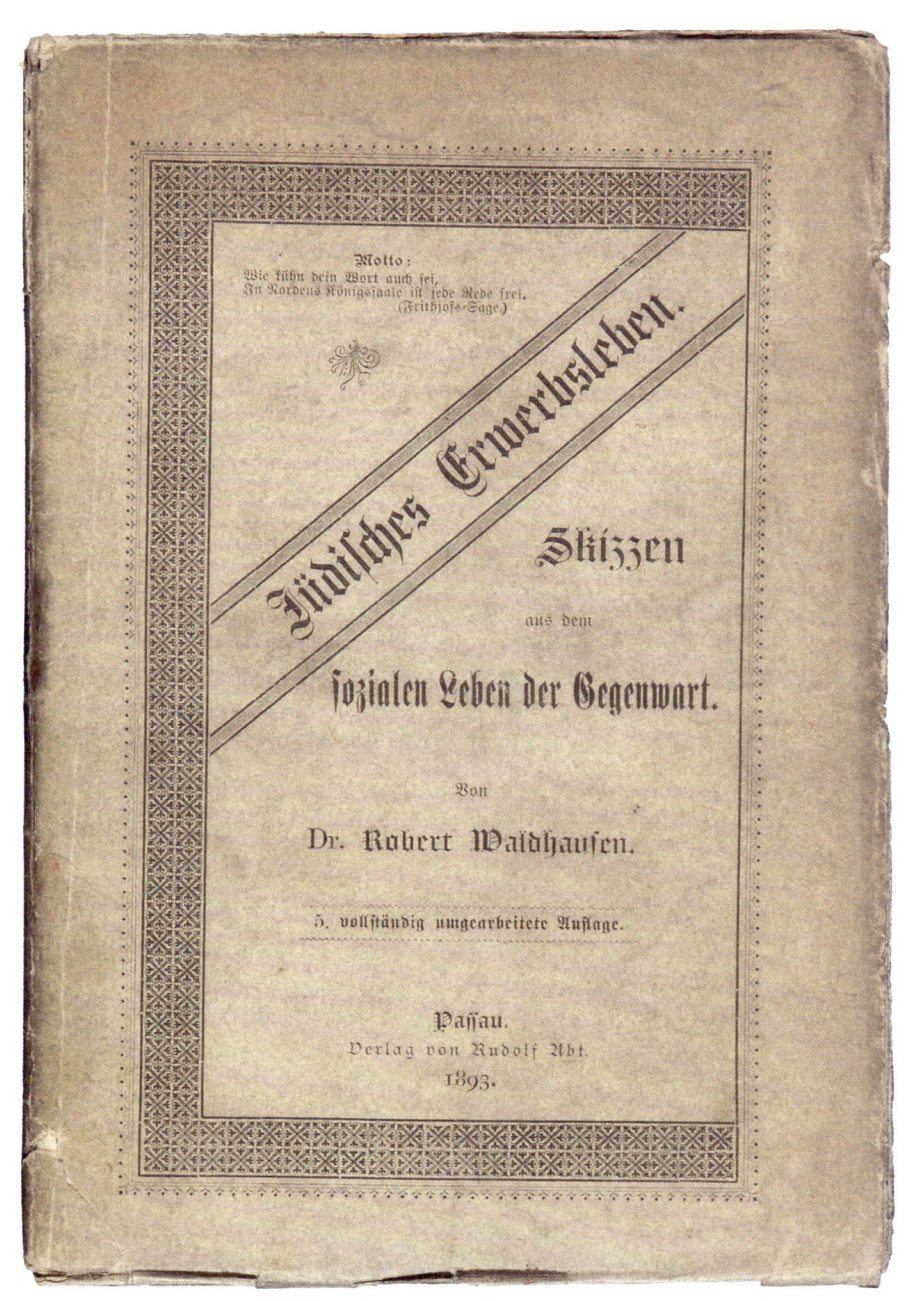

9
Jüdisches Erwerbsleben.
Skizzen aus dem sozialen Leben der Gegenwart
Dr. Robert Waldhausen
(d.i. Georg Ratzinger, 1844–1899)
Passau, 1893
Druck
8°

Jüdisches Museum München

9
Jewish Working Life:
Sketches from the Society of Today
Dr. Robert Waldhausen
(pseudonym of Georg Ratzinger, 1844–99)
Passau, 1893
Printed pamphlet
8°

Jewish Museum Munich

Verfolgung und Vernichtung 1933–1945

Nach der Machtergreifung der Nationalsozialisten 1933 wurden die Diskriminierung von Juden und ihre Ausgrenzung aus der deutschen Gesellschaft zur staatlichen Politik. Menschen wurden in den Folgejahren aussortiert, deportiert und ermordet. Die Verdrängung aus dem Berufsleben führte zum Verlust der wirtschaftlichen Existenz. Nach der Zerstörung der Synagogen 1938 wurden Enteignungen und Verfolgungen systematisch betrieben. Möglichkeiten zur Emigration bestanden danach kaum noch. Von den über 10.000 jüdischen Münchnern wurden mehr als 3.000 deportiert und ermordet.

Das Ehepaar Rosa und Louis Picard hatte 1900 im Rückgebäude der Landwehrstraße 44 die Firma Louis Picard OHG gegründet, die Wäsche und Schürzen herstellte und auch Weiß- und Wollwaren vertrieb. Die beiden Söhne Max und Heinrich wurden Teilhaber im Familienbetrieb.

1938 verlor Max Picard wie alle jüdischen Handelsreisenden seine Gewerbekarte, da der Münchner Oberbürgermeister Karl Fiehler deren jährlich notwendige Ausstellung verweigerte. Als sich der Druck auf jüdische Unternehmen erhöhte, war die Familie gezwungen, ihr Warenlager an die Firma Büttel & Railling in der Sendlinger Straße 70 zu verkaufen, die dann auch alle 30 Mitarbeiter übernahm.

Rosa Picard und ihr Ehemann Louis versuchten noch, im September 1939 nach England zu emigrieren. Doch nur ihrem Sohn Max gelang es ein Jahr später, in die USA zu fliehen. Sein Bruder Heinrich und dessen Frau wurden mit dem ersten Transport von jüdischen Münchnern 1941 nach Litauen deportiert und unmittelbar nach der Ankunft in Kaunas erschossen. Rosa Picard verstarb 1941 in München, ihr Mann Louis wurde 1942 nach Theresienstadt verschleppt und dort ermordet.

Zurück blieb Rosa Picards gepackter Überseekoffer, den sie nach 1938 der befreundeten christlichen Familie Max und Luise Geyer in München zur Verwahrung anvertraut hatte. Später ging der Koffer in den Besitz der Tochter über. Deren ältester Sohn Dr. Hubert Engelbrecht überbrachte den Koffer – inzwischen ohne Inhalt – 2001 dem Jüdischen Museum.

Eine Großnichte Rosa Picards bestimmte 2006, dass der Koffer als Leihgabe im Jüdischen Museum verbleiben soll.

[J.Fl.]

Persecution and Mass Murder, 1933–1945

After the National Socialists seized power in 1933, the discrimination of Jews in Germany and their exclusion from society was part of government policy. In the years to follow, Jews were subjected to selection procedures, deported, and murdered. Being forced to give up their professions led to the loss of their financial existence. The destruction of the synagogues in 1938 was followed by misappropriation and systematic persecution. From that time onward, emigration became virtually impossible. Of the 10,000 Jews still living in Munich at that time, 3,000 were deported and murdered.

The couple Rosa and Louis Picard had founded the company Louis Picard OHG in 1900 in a building at the back of Landwehrstrasse 44. They produced underwear and aprons, and sold linen and woollen goods. Both sons, Max and Heinrich, became associated partners in the family business.

In 1938, Max Picard loss his trading licence, as did all Jewish salespeople—the Lord Mayor of Munich, Karl Fiehler, having refused to allow their crucial annual trade fair to take place. As pressure on Jewish businesses increased, the family was forced to sell its stock to the company Büttel & Railling at Sendlinger Strasse 70, who also took on the 30 members of staff.

Rosa Picard and her husband Louis tried to emigrate to England in September 1939. However, only their son Max succeeded to flee to the USA one year later. His brother Heinrich and sister-in-law were deported to Lithuania on the first trainload of Jews from Munich in 1941, and were shot immediately after their arrival in Kaunas. Rosa Picard died in Munich in 1941; her husband was deported to Theresienstadt in 1942 where he was murdered.

Rosa Picard's packed trunk, which she had given to the befriended Christian family of Max and Luise Geyer in Munich for safe-keeping, was left behind. The trunk later came into the daughter's possession. Her eldest son, Dr. Hubert Engelbrecht, presented the now empty trunk to the Jewish Museum in 2001.

In 2006, the daughter of Rosa Picard's nephew requested that the trunk remain as a permanent loan in the Jewish Museum.

Andreas Heusler
Historiker \ Historian

„Viele haben versucht, sich ins Ausland zu retten. Allerdings waren die Emigrationsbemühungen für viele zum Scheitern verurteilt. Etwa 3.000 Münchner Juden wurden ab 1941 aus der Stadt in verschiedene Todes- und Vernichtungslager, auch in das so genannte Prominenten-Ghetto in Theresienstadt, deportiert. Als im April 1945 amerikanische Soldaten München besetzten, war die Jüdische Gemeinde dieser Stadt, die einstmals sehr blühend gewesen war und sehr viele kulturelle und wirtschaftliche Akzente gesetzt hatte, verschwunden."

"Many tried to flee abroad, but attempts to emigrate were often doomed to failure. Some 3,000 Jews from Munich were deported to different death and extermination camps in 1941, as well as to the so-called "Prominenten" ghetto in Theresienstadt for Jews of a higher social status. When American troops occupied Munich in April 1945, the Jewish community, which once flourished and played such an important role in the cultural and economic life of the city, had disappeared."

10
Übersee-Koffer
Leipzig, um 1920
Rohrflachsplatte, Leinen, Leder, Metall
Hersteller: Firma Mädler, Leipzig
H: 142 cm, B: 52 cm, T: 42 cm

Privatbesitz

Die Initialen R.P. finden sich seitlich
auf dem Überseekoffer aufgedruckt und
verweisen auf die letzte Eigentümerin
Rosa Picard.

10
Trunk
Leipzig, c. 1920
Flax cloth casing, linen, leather, metal
Manufacturer: Mädler, Leipzig
H: 142 cm, W: 52 cm, D: 42 cm

Private collection

R.P., printed on the side of the trunk,
are the initials of the trunk's last owner,
Rosa Picard.

München als „Zwischenort" für Überlebende nach 1945

In den Jahren 1945 bis 1951 wurde München zum „Zwischenort" für jüdische Überlebende der Konzentrationslager und der Todesmärsche, für Partisanen und bis in die Weiten der ehemaligen Sowjetunion Geflohene. Sie kamen in die amerikanische Besatzungszone – nach München. Die frühere „Hauptstadt der Bewegung" wurde für einige Jahre zum Zentrum der Sche'erit Hapleta, dem geretteten Rest.

Die jüdischen Displaced Persons (DPs), Überlebende aus Osteuropa, wurden in DP-Camps wie etwa in Neu-Freimann, Landsberg, Feldafing und Föhrenwald untergebracht. In Bogenhausen hatten viele Hilfsorganisationen ihre Büros, und der Münchner Stadtteil wurde so in der unmittelbaren Nachkriegszeit zur Anlaufstelle für Zehntausende von Juden auf dem Weg in ihre Zielländer.

Das American Jewish Joint Distribution Committee (JOINT) eröffnete nach Kriegsende in München seinen europäischen Hauptsitz. Die amerikanisch-jüdische Hilfsorganisation, die in der Siebertstraße 3 untergebracht war, richtete Suchdienste ein und verteilte Lebensmittel und Kleidung. Sie förderte berufliche Ausbildungen und finanzierte neben DP-Zeitungen drei jiddische Theater und zwei DP-Orchester. Der JOINT druckte mehr als 500.000 Gebetbücher, ließ Mazzot backen, verteilte Gebetsriemen und -mäntel, Schofarim und Mesusot, um ein religiöses Leben in den Camps zu ermöglichen.

Der Seder-Teller entstammt einer Produktion des JOINT Employment Boards im Jahr 1947. Das Pessach-Fest als Erinnerung an die Befreiung aus der Sklaverei in Ägypten hatte für die Überlebenden der Schoa eine besondere Bedeutung. Der Wunsch „Nächstes Jahr in Jerusalem", der zu Pessach am Ende jeder Seder-Feier steht, findet sich auf dem Teller mit „Dieses Jahr in Jerusalem" und spiegelt die Sehnsucht vieler DPs nach einem schnellen Ende des Provisoriums auf deutschem Boden wider.

Von München aus wurden diese Seder-Teller mitgenommen – nach Israel wie nach Nordamerika. Dort begann für viele der Displaced Persons ein neues Leben.

Munich as a "Stop-over Point" for Survivors, after 1945

Between 1945 and 1951, Munich became a "stop-over point" for Jewish survivors of concentration camps and death marches, for partisans, and those who had fled deep into the former Soviet Union. They all came to the American occupation zone, to Munich. For just a few years, what was once the "Capital of the Movement" became the centre of the *She'erit Hapleta*, "the Remainder of the Saved."

The Jewish survivors from eastern Europe, or "Displaced Persons" (DPs), were accommodated in DP camps such as in Neu-Freimann, Landsberg, Feldafing, and Föhrenwald. Many aid organisations had their offices in Bogenhausen, and immediately after the War this district of Munich was sought out by tens of thousands of Jews on their way to the countries where they wanted to settle.

The American Jewish Joint Distribution Committee (JOINT) opened its European headquarters in Munich at the end of the War. The American-Jewish charity at Siebertstrasse 3 provided a tracing service and distributed food and clothing. It funded professional training and financed three Yiddish theaters and two DP orchestras, in addition to DP newspapers. JOINT printed more than 500,000 prayer books, baked *matzot*, distributed prayer belts and shawls, *shofarim* and *mezuzot*, to enable the practice of religious rites in the camps.

The *Seder* plate was produced by the JOINT Employment Board in 1947. The Passover Feast, as a reminder of being liberated from slavery in Egypt, gained a poignant new meaning for survivors of the *Shoah*. The wish said at the end of every *Seder* Feast: "Next year in Jerusalem," has been adapted to "This year in Jerusalem" on this plate, reflecting the yearning of many DPs for an end to their provisional status on German territory.

These *Seder* plates were taken from Munich to Israel and North America, where many displaced persons started a new life.

[J.Fl.]

Jim G. Tobias
Historiker \ Historian

„Eine Zukunft in Deutschland war für die überlebenden Juden unvorstellbar. Sehnsüchtig warteten sie darauf, dass der Staat Israel gegründet würde. Im Mai 1948 war es endlich so weit. Dort fand eine überwiegende Mehrheit der in Deutschland gestrandeten Juden, die hier in den Wartesälen, den DP-Camps, lebten, eine neue Heimat. Andere suchten ihr Glück in den Vereinigten Staaten, in Kanada, Australien oder England."

"A future in Germany was unthinkable for those Jews who had survived. They longingly waited for the founding of the State of Israel. In May 1948, their wait was over, and the vast majority of Jews stranded in Germany and living in 'waiting rooms,' the camps for Displaced Persons, started a new life there. Others tried their luck in the United States, Canada, Australia, or England."

**11
Seder-Teller**
München, 1947
Steingut, glasiert
Hersteller: JOINT Employment Board
D: 30 cm

Jüdisches Museum München, # JM 05/2004

**11
Seder Plate**
Munich, 1947
Stoneware, glazed
Manufacturer: JOINT Employment Board
Diameter: 30 cm

Jewish Museum Munich, # JM 05/2004

„Bitte kehrt zurück, wenn Ihr wollt"   "Please come back if you want"

Je weiter die Zeit des Nationalsozialismus und der Holocaust zeitlich in die Ferne rücken, umso stärker treten die Versuche, Orte des Erinnerns zu formen, ins Blickfeld des öffentlichen Interesses. Den Prozess der Planung und Erbauung von Mahnmalen und Museen begleiten regelmäßig heftige Kontroversen über die Möglichkeiten und Grenzen von Denkmalkunst im öffentlichen Raum und eine angemessene Form der künstlerischen Darstellung.

Die beiden Münchner Künstler Rudolf Herz und Thomas Lehnerer versuchten im Frühjahr 1990 mit einer vorher nicht offiziell angekündigten Kunstaktion an historischer Stätte, die Frage nach dem Ort und der Wirksamkeit von Kunst im öffentlichen Raum noch einmal neu zu stellen. Am Morgen des 13. März befestigten sie an der Feldherrnhalle ein Schild mit der Aufschrift „Juden in aller Welt bitte kehrt zurück, wenn Ihr wollt." Das Schild sollte zugleich Mahnmal und Ausdruck einer ehrlichen Bitte sein: „Denn wer verstoßen wurde, den muß man wieder zurückbitten. Dies ist bisher öffentlich und in verbindlicher Weise nicht geschehen", so Rudolf Herz und Thomas Lehnerer in einer öffentlichen Stellungnahme. Schon nach weniger als zwei Stunden musste das Schild auf behördliche Anordnung entfernt werden. Ein Schreiben der Künstler, gerichtet an den Freistaat Bayern und die offiziellen Stellen der Stadt München, begleitete die Aktion und zog eine öffentliche Debatte nach sich.

Der Ort für die Anbringung des Schildes war bewusst gewählt. Denn die Feldherrnhalle, ein unter Ludwig I. errichtetes Ehrenmal für die Bayerische Armee und deren siegreiche Feldherren, war keineswegs nur Monument des 19. Jahrhunderts, sondern hatte als Kultstätte der NSDAP während des „Dritten Reichs" eine große ideologische Bedeutung, die nach 1945 von der Stadt München weitgehend verdrängt wurde. Mit ihrer Kunstaktion wollten Lehnerer und Herz auch diesen Aspekt der Stadtgeschichte wieder ins öffentliche Bewusstsein rücken.

Das Schild sollte nicht nur an die beschämende deutsche Vergangenheit erinnern, die Künstler formulierten damit auch einen Wunsch für die Zukunft und kehrten so die übliche Ausrichtung eines Mahnmals um. Gerade die ablehnenden und ausweichenden Reaktionen von offizieller Seite aber zeigen, dass die Stadt München im Jahr 1990 für eine so offensive Strategie des Gedenkens, wie Lehnerer und Herz sie vertraten, keinen Platz zu haben schien.

The further National Socialism and the Holocaust fade into the past, the more striking the attempts to create places of remembrance and to bring them to the attention of the general public. The process of planning and building monuments and museums is regularly accompanied by fierce controversy about the possibilities and limits of memorial art in the public domain and the most appropriate manner of artistic representation.

The two Munich artists Rudolf Herz and Thomas Lehnerer wanted to raise the question once again as to the positioning and effectivity of art in public spaces with their inofficial art event in spring 1990 at an historical site. Early on March 13, they fixed a sign to the Feldherrnhalle (The Field Marshals' Hall) which read: "Jews from around the world, please come back, if you want to." The sign was meant as both a memorial and an expression of a genuine request: "After all, if someone has been turned away, he has to be asked to come back. This has never been done publicly and bindingly." This was Rudolf Herz and Thomas Lehnerer's explanation. In less than two hours, the sign had been officially removed. A letter by the artists to the Free State of Bavaria and to the respective office of the City of Munich, accompanied this event and launched a public debate.

The place where the sign was hung was carefully chosen. The Feldherrnhalle, erected under Ludwig I in honor of the Bavarian army and its victorious field marshals, was not merely a 19th-century monument but had considerable ideological significance as an NSDAP cult site during the Third Reich—something that has largely been suppressed by the City of Munich since 1945. Lehnerer and Herz also wanted to re-awaken public awareness of this aspect in the city's history with their art event.

The sign was not only intended as a reminder of a shameful past; the artists were also expressing a wish for the future and were turning the usual form of a memorial the other way round. The reaction from the official side, which was one of denial and avoidance of the issue, showed that the City of Munich in 1990 appeared not to be open to such an offensive commemorative strategy as that of Lehnerer and Herz.

[U.He.]

„Dieses Denkmal ist ein besonderes Denkmal. Es beklagt keine Schuld, wie wir dies üblicherweise haben, wenn an die Verbrechen der Deutschen zur Zeit des Nationalsozialismus erinnert wird. Es stellt den Verlust fest, der der deutschen Gesellschaft zugefügt worden ist durch die Vertreibung und die Ermordung der Juden. Das Zweite, was dieses Denkmal an Besonderem hat, ist, dass es ein geschenktes Denkmal ist. Während sonst der Staat fürsorglich für die Bürger arbeitet und auch ihre Denkmäler und ihr Geschichtsbewusstsein versucht zu konstruieren, haben sich die beiden Künstler entschlossen, ein Denkmal an die Wand anzuheften, wo der Verbrecher selber gedacht wurde."

"This memorial is a special one. It is not apportioning blame, as is usually the case whenever we are reminded of the crimes committed by the Germans under the National Socialists. It establishes a loss forced on German society through the persecution and murder of Jews. The second thing that makes this memorial special is that is was a gift. While the state may work caringly for its citizens, build monuments and create an historical awareness, the two artists decided to fix their own memorial to a wall at a place where the Criminal himself was remembered."

Detlef Hoffmann
Kunsthistoriker
\ Art Historian

12
Schild an der Feldherrnhalle 1990
Rudolf Herz (*1954) und
Thomas Lehnerer (1955-1995)
München, 1990
Eisenblech, emailliert
H: 35 cm, B: 45 cm

Leihgabe Rudolf Herz und Archiv Thomas Lehnerer

12
Sign on the Feldherrnhalle 1990
Rudolf Herz (*1954) and
Thomas Lehnerer (1955-95)
Munich, 1990
Sheet iron, enameled
H: 35 cm, W: 45 cm

Loan of Rudolf Herz and Archive Thomas Lehnerer

Videotafeln für die Ausstellung „Stadt ohne Juden"

Für die Ausstellung „Stadt ohne Juden" bat das Jüdische Museum München zwölf Fachleute vor die Kamera, um die einzelnen Exponate zu beschreiben und in einen größeren Kontext zu setzen. Das Ergebnis sind ‚Videotafeln', die diese Objekte historisch und geografisch einordnen.

Die Arbeiten entstanden zwischen Mai und September 2008 in Zusammenarbeit mit den Mitarbeitern des Jüdischen Museums und der Hochschule für Fernsehen und Film in München. Unter der Leitung von Prof. Heiner Stadler erarbeiteten fünf Studierende der Abteilung Dokumentarfilm und Fernsehpublizistik ein Konzept, das an Originalschauplätzen und im Studio der Hochschule für Fernsehen und Film umgesetzt wurde.

Bei ihrer Aufgabe, Experten und Orte in einem Bild zusammenzubringen, entschieden sich die Regiestudenten gegen die nahe liegende Kombination am Drehort. Stattdessen wurden Experten und Orte separat aufgenommen und erst in der Postproduktion durch das Übereinanderlegen beider Bildebenen kombiniert: im Vordergrund der Experte, im Hintergrund der jeweilige Ort. Die Filme wurden im Hochformat realisiert, um ihren Charakter als Variante klassischer Museumstexte zu unterstreichen.

Die Plätze in München wurden in Farbe mit Super-8-Film aufgenommen. Die typischen Charakteristika des Materials – warme Farben und Grobkörnigkeit – vermitteln einen Eindruck von der Diskrepanz zwischen der Gegenwart der Filmaufnahme und der erzählten Vergangenheit.

Die knapp zwei Minuten langen Einzelstatements wurden schwarz-weiß auf Video (HD) gedreht. Der Kontrast ist stark angehoben, feinere Konturen verschwinden. Diese Verfremdung betont den Inhalt des Textes und nicht die kommentierende Person. Als Verweis auf die Fragmentierung jüdischen Lebens in der Münchner Stadtgeschichte wurden unterschiedliche Einstellungsgrößen gewählt und die Fachleute zum Teil dekadriert, also absichtlich angeschnitten und deplatziert.

Projektgruppe „Stadt ohne Juden"
Hochschule für Fernsehen und Film München

Video Boards for the Exhibition "City without Jews"

As part of the exhibition "City without Jews," The Jewish Museum Munich asked twelve experts to describe the individual objects in front of the camera and to place them in their wider context. These video boards, which give the exhibits an historical and geographical anchor, are the result.

The boards were created between May and September 2008 as a coproduction between the Jewish Museum Munich and the University for Television and Film Munich. Under Prof. Heiner Stadler's guidance, five students from the department of Documentary Film and Television Journalism worked out a concept which was realised at the original locations and in the university's own studio.

The film students decided against combining the experts and the locations in one take, as would have been the easiest way. Instead, the two were filmed separately and only brought together in the post-production stage by superimposing one image on the other: with the experts in the foreground and the respective locations in the background. The films were made using a portrait format, as a way of underlining their character as a variant to the classic style of museum text.

The locations in Munich were captured in color on Super-8 film. The typical features of this medium—warm colors and a coarse structure—convey the impression of a discrepancy between the present (the film pictures) and the (related) past.

Each statement lasts just under two minutes and has been filmed on HD video in black and white. The contrast has been greatly exaggerated and delicate contours removed. This alienation emphasises the content of the texts and not the commentator. Varying setting sizes were chosen to reflect the fragmentary character of Jewish life in Munich's history, with the experts being partially cut out of the frame and moved off center intentionally.

Project group "City without Jews"
University of Television and Film Munich

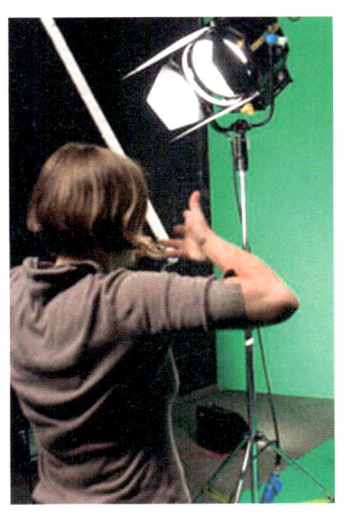

Bibliografie
Bibliography

1
Ritualmord-Vorwurf und Pogrom 1285
Accusations of Ritual Murder and Pogrom in 1285

Barzen, Rainer: Anfänge im Mittelalter (1229–1442), in: Bauer, Richard; Brenner, Michael (Hg.): Jüdisches München. Vom Mittelalter bis zur Gegenwart, München 2006, 21-38.

Heimann-Jelinek, Felicitas: Memorbücher: „Milieux de mémoire", in: Purin, Bernhard (Hg.): Buch der Erinnerung. Das Wiener Memorbuch der Fürther Klaus-Synagoge, Fürth 1999, 27-38.

Pomerance, Aubrey: „Bekannt in den Toren". Name und Nachruf in Memorbüchern, in: Hödl, Sabine; Lappin, Eleonore (Hg.): Erinnerung als Gegenwart. Jüdische Gedenkkulturen, Wien 2000, 33-53.

Weinberg, Magnus: Das Memorbuch, in: Purin, Bernhard (Hg.): Buch der Erinnerung. Das Wiener Memorbuch der Fürther Klaus-Synagoge, Fürth 1999, 9-26.

2
Ritualmord-Vorwurf 1346
Accusation of Ritual Murder in 1346

Die Macht der Bilder: Antisemitische Vorurteile und Mythen, Ausstellungskatalog (Jüdisches Museum der Stadt Wien), Wien 1995.

Erb, Rainer (Hg.): Die Legende vom Ritualmord. Zur Geschichte der Blutbeschuldigung gegen Juden, Berlin 1993.

Schreckenberg, Heinz: Die Juden in der Kunst Europas, Göttingen 1996.

3
Hostienfrevel-Beschuldigung 1349
Accusation of Host Desecration in 1349

Bauerreiss, Romuald: Pie Jesu. Das Schmerzensmann-Bild und sein Einfluß auf die mittelalterliche Frömmigkeit, München 1931, 33.

Mittlmeier, Christine: Publizistik im Dienste antijüdischer Polemik. Spätmittelalterliche und frühneuzeitliche Flugschriften und Flugblätter zu Hostienschändungen (= Mikrokosmos. Beiträge zur Literaturwissenschaft und Bedeutungsforschung 56), Frankfurt/M. 2000.

Stahleder, Helmut: Chronik der Stadt München. Die Jahre 1157–1505, München 1995, 226-227.

4
Umwandlung der Synagoge in eine Kirche 1442
Conversion of Synagogue to a Church in 1442

Gufler, Jakob: Ergänzungen und Berichtigungen zu dem im Jahrg. 1867 dieses Kalenders Seite 41-45 enthaltenen Artikel I.: „Die ehemalige Gruftkirche am Gruftgäßchen in München", in: Kalender für katholische Christen auf das Schaltjahr 1868, Sulzbach 1867, 120-122.

Merback, Mitchell B.: Cleansing the Temple: The Munich Gruftkirche as Converted Synagogue, in: Merback, Mitchell B. (Ed.): Beyond the Yellow Badge. Anti-Judaism and Antisemitism in Medieval and Early Modern Visual Culture, Leiden-Boston 2008, 305-345.

Scharl, Placidus; Sattler, Markus: Die ehemalige Gruftkirche am Gruftgäßchen in München, in: Kalender für katholische Christen auf das Jahr 1867, Sulzbach 1866, 41-45.

Schneid, Konrad: Rückkehr der Salmdorfer Pietà und Wiedereröffnung der Salmdorfer Kirche. Dokumentation, Haar 2003.

Steiner, Peter B.; Karbacher, Rupert: Vesperbild von Salmdorf, in: Madonna. Das Bild der Muttergottes, Ausstellungskatalog (Diözesanmuseum Freising), Freising-Lindenberg 2003, 186-188.

5
Judenpolitik Herzog Albrechts V. im 16. Jahrhundert
The Jewish Policy of Duke Albrecht V in the 16th Century

Heil, Dietmar: Die Reichspolitik Bayerns unter der Regierung Herzog Albrechts V. (1550-1579), Göttingen 1998.

Heimers, Manfred Peter: Aufenthaltsverbot und eingeschränkte Zulassung (1442-1799), in: Bauer, Richard; Brenner, Michael (Hg.): Jüdisches München. Vom Mittelalter bis zur Gegenwart, München 2006, 39-57.

Staudinger, Barbara: Sammelbilder 01: Die jüdische Welt und die Wittelsbacher, Ausstellungskatalog (Jüdisches Museum München), München 2007.

6
Ahasver, der Ewige Jude in München
Ahasver, the Wandering Jew in Munich

Apollinaire, Guillaume: Le Passant de Prague, in: L'Hérésiarque et Cie, Paris 1910.

Cohen, Richard I.: The „Wandering Jew" from Medieval Legend to Modern Metaphor, in: Kirshenblatt-Gimblett, Barbara; Karp, Jonathan: The Art of Being Jewish in Modern Times, Philadelphia 2008, 147-175.

Feuchtwanger, Lion: Gespräche mit dem Ewigen Juden, in: An den Wassern von Babylon. Ein fast heiteres Judenbuch, München 1920, 53-92.

Körte, Mona: Die Uneinholbarkeit des Verfolgten. Der Ewige Jude in der literarischen Phantastik, Frankfurt/M. 2000.

Ronen, Avraham: Kaulbach's Wandering Jew: An Anti-Jewish Allegory and Two Jewish Responses, in: Assaph. Studies in Art History 3 (1998), 243-263.

7
Juden als geduldete Geldgeber im 18. Jahrhundert
Jews as Tolerated Moneylenders in the 18th Century

Heimers, Manfred Peter: Aufenthaltsverbot und eingeschränkte Zulassung (1442-1799), in: Bauer, Richard; Brenner, Michael (Hg.): Jüdisches München. Vom Mittelalter bis zur Gegenwart, München 2006, 39-57.

Kaufmann, David: Samson Wertheimer, der Oberhoffactor und Landesrabbiner 1658-1724 und seine Brüder, Wien 1888.

Stern, Selma: Der Hofjude im Zeitalter des Absolutismus. Ein Beitrag zur europäischen Geschichte im 17. und 18. Jahrhundert, hg. von Marina Sassenberg, Tübingen 2001.

8
Taufe als Entre Billet in die Gesellschaft um 1800
Baptism as Entry Ticket to Society, c. 1800

Kilian, Hendrikje: Die jüdische Gemeinde in München 1813-1871. Eine Großstadtgemeinde im Zeitalter der Emanzipation, München 1989.

Lässig, Simone: Jüdische Wege ins Bürgertum. Kulturelles Kapital und sozialer Aufstieg im 19. Jahrhundert, Göttingen 2004.

Maggid, David: Zur Geschichte der Familien Günzburg, St. Petersburg 1899 [hebr.].

Minden, Georg: Die Thorah-Wimpel oder Mappe. Ein Beitrag zur jüdischen Volkskunde, in: Zeitschrift des Vereins für Volkskunde 2 (1893), 205-208.

Weber, Annette; Friedlander, Evelyn; Armbruster, Fritz: Mappot ... gesegnet, der da kommt. Das Band jüdischer Tradition, Ausstellungskatalog, Osnabrück 1997.

9
Katholischer Antisemitismus um 1900
Catholic Anti-Semitism, c. 1900

Blaschke, Olaf: Katholizismus und Antisemitismus im Deutschen Kaiserreich, Göttingen 1997.

Blaschke, Olaf; Mattioli, Aram (Hg.): Katholischer Antisemitismus im 19. Jahrhundert. Ursachen und Tradition im internationalen Vergleich, Zürich 2000.

Kirchinger, Johann; Schütz, Ernst (Hg.): Georg Ratzinger (1844-1899). Ein Leben zwischen Politik, Geschichte und Seelsorge, Regensburg 2008.

Ludyga, Hannes: Die Rechtsstellung der Juden in Bayern von 1819 bis 1918. Studie im Spiegel der Verhandlungen der Kammer der Abgeordneten des bayerischen Landtags, Berlin 2007.

10
Verfolgung und Vernichtung 1933-1945
Persecution and Mass Murder, 1933-1945

Baumann, Angelika; Heusler, Andreas (Hg.): München arisiert. Entrechtung und Enteignung der Juden in der NS-Zeit, München 2004.

Selig, Wolfram: „Arisierung" in München. Die Vernichtung jüdischer Existenz 1937-1939, Berlin 2004, 792-793.

Münchner Stadtarchiv (Hg.): Biographisches Gedenkbuch der Münchner Juden 1933-1945, Bd. 2, München 2007, 252-255.

11
München als „Zwischenort" für Überlebende nach 1945
Munich as a "Stop-over Point" for Survivors, after 1945

Diner, Dan: Erinnerungsort München, in: Tworek, Elisabeth: „... und dazwischen ein schöner Rausch". Dichter und Künstler aus aller Welt in München, München 2008, 82-83.

Kauders, Anthony D.; Lewinsky, Tamar: Neuanfang mit Zweifeln (1945-1970), in: Bauer, Richard; Brenner, Michael (Hg.): Jüdisches München. Vom Mittelalter bis zur Gegenwart, München 2006, 185-208.

Königseder, Angelika; Wetzel, Juliane: Lebensmut im Wartesaal. Die jüdischen DPs (Displaced Persons) im Nachkriegsdeutschland, Frankfurt 2004.

AJDC Organizational Structure, U.S. Zone Germany, in: American Jewish Joint Distribution Comitee: AJDC Operations in U.S. Zone Germany 1948, ed. Harold Kempner, Munich 1948, 4.

12
„Bitte kehrt zurück, wenn Ihr wollt"
"Please come back if you want"

Herz, Rudolf; Lehnerer, Thomas: Schild an der Feldherrnhalle. Dokumentation, München 1990.

Kunz-Ott, Hannelore; Kluge, Andrea (Hg.): 150 Jahre Feldherrnhalle. Lebensraum einer Großstadt, München 1994.

Rosenfeld, Gavriel D.: Architektur und Gedächtnis. München und Nationalsozialismus. Strategien des Vergessens, München 2004.

Young, James E.: Nach-Bilder des Holocaust in zeitgenössischer Kunst und Architektur, Hamburg 2001.

Stadt ohne Juden –
Die Nachtseite der
Münchner Stadtgeschichte
\ City without Jews –
The Dark Side of Munich's History

Eine Ausstellung des
Jüdischen Museums München
24. September 2008
bis 30. August 2009
\ An exhibition organized by the
Jewish Museum Munich
September 24, 2008
to August 30, 2009

IDEE UND KONZEPT
\ IDEA AND CONCEPT
Bernhard Purin

MITARBEIT
\ CURATORIAL ASSISTANCE
Tatjana Neef

AUTOREN
\ AUTORS
Jutta Fleckenstein (J.Fl.)
Ulrike Heikaus (U.He.)
Tatjana Neef (T.Ne.)
Bernhard Purin (B.Pu.)
Dr. Barbara Staudinger (B.St.)

KOORDINATION
\ COORDINATION
Verena Immler

AUSSTELLUNGSGESTALTUNG
\ EXHIBITION DESIGN
Architekt Martin Kohlbauer

REALISIERUNG
\ REALIZATION
Architekt Christian Koch

AUSSTELLUNGSGRAFIK
\ EXHIBITION GRAPHICS
Haller & Haller

RESTAURATORISCHE BETREUUNG
\ CONSERVATOR
Klaus Büchel

AUSSTELLUNGSPRODUKTION
\ EXHIBITION PRODUCTION
Hasan Güneri
Sabine Menges

LEIHGEBER
\ LENDERS
Bayerisches Nationalmuseum,
München

Bayerische Staatsbibliothek,
München

Diözesanmuseum Freising

Filialkirchenstiftung Maria
Himmelfahrt Salmdorf in der Pfarrei
Ottendichl, Gemeinde Haar

Rudolf Herz und Archiv Thomas
Lehnerer, München

Jüdisches Museum der Stadt Wien

Metropolitankapitel Zu Unserer
Lieben Frau, München

DANK
\ ACKNOWLEDGMENTS

Dr. Karl Albrecht-Weinberger
Jüdisches Museum der Stadt Wien

Margot Attenkofer
München

Margarita Balaklav
Sam Spiegel Film & Television School Jerusalem

Bargig Family
Tel Aviv

Dr. Richard Bauer
Münchner Stadtarchiv

Regina Bauer-Empl
Diözesanmuseum Freising

Doris Dörrie
München

Dr. Renate Eikelmann
Bayerisches Nationalmuseum, München

Dr. Hubert Engelbrecht
München

Sergeij Freedmann
Tel Aviv University

Dr. Brigitte Gullath
Bayerische Staatsbibliothek, München

Dr. Sylvia Hahn
Diözesanmuseum Freising

Dr. Felicitas Heimann-Jelinek
Jüdisches Museum der Stadt Wien

Rupert Karbacher
Landesamt für Denkmalpflege, München

Dr. Norbert Jocher
Kunstreferat des Erzbistums München und Freising

Boris Levine
HFF Gerätetechnik

Dr. Otto Lohr
Landesstelle für die nichtstaatlichen Museen in Bayern

Andreas von Majewski
Wittelsbacher Ausgleichsfonds München

Gerhard Milchram
Jüdisches Museum der Stadt Wien

Dr. Peter Pfister
Archiv des Erzbistums München und Freising

Christiane Picard
München

Sylvia Pitum
Bayerische Staatsbibliothek, München

Dorothea Preyss
München

Christa Prokisch
Jüdisches Museum der Stadt Wien

Pfarrer Albert Schamberger
Salmdorf

Dr. Astrid Scherp
Bayerisches Nationalmuseum, München

Dr. Ingo Schwab
Münchner Stadtarchiv

Dr. Wolfgang Till
Münchner Stadtmuseum

Guido Treffler
Archiv des Erzbistums München und Freising

Philip Vogt
Berlin

Wolfgang Wastian
München

Dr. Alexander Wiessmann
Landesstelle für die nichtstaatlichen Museen in Bayern

Domdekan Dr. Lorenz Wolf
Metropolitankapitel München

VIDEOTAFELN
\ VIDEO BOARDS

Eine Koproduktion der Hochschule für Fernsehen und Film München und des Jüdischen Museums München
\ A Coproduction with the University of Television and Film Munich and the Jewish Museum Munich

KOMMENTATOREN
\ COMMENTATORS

Prof. Dr. Wolfgang Brückner
Universität Würzburg

Prof. Dr. Richard I. Cohen
Hebrew University, Jerusalem

Prof. Dr. Winfried Frey
Universität Frankfurt/M.

Dr. Kurt Greussing
Dornbirn

Dr. Dietmar Heil
Historische Kommission bei der Bayerischen Akademie der Wissenschaften, Regensburg

Dr. Andreas Heusler
Münchner Stadtarchiv

Prof. Dr. Detlef Hoffmann
Universität Oldenburg

Prof. Dr. Rolf Kießling
Universität Augsburg

Dr. Christine Mittlmeier
München

Aubrey Pomerance
Archiv des Jüdischen Museums Berlin

Bernhard Purin
Jüdisches Museum München

Jim G. Tobias
Nürnberger Institut für NS-Forschung und jüdische Geschichte des 20. Jahrhunderts

REGIE
\ DIRECTION

Katrin Jäger
Franziska von Malsen-Ponickau
Lena Stahl
Johanna Thalmann
Steffen Weber

BILDGESTALTUNG
\ COMPOSITION

Sanne Kurz

KAMERAASSISTENZ UND LICHT
\ CAMERA ASSISTANCE AND LIGHTING

Haim Bargig

TON
\ SOUND

Ali Zojaji
Lena Stahl
Johanna Thalmann
Steffen Weber

AUFNAHMELEITUNG
\ PRODUCTION MANAGEMENT

Katrin Jäger
Franziska von Malsen-Ponickau

MASKE
\ MAKE-UP

Paulina Pavlik

SCHNITT, COMPOSITING UND ENDFERTIGUNG
\ CUT, COMPOSITING AND FINISHING

Uwe Wrobel

SUPER-8-ENTWICKLUNG
\ SUPER 8 DEVELOPING

Andec Filmtechnik Berlin

SUPER-8-ABTASTUNG
\ SUPER 8 SCANNING

Berola Film Forchheim
Dirk Jurschewsky

SPRECHERIN
\ NARRATOR

Helen Simon

STANDFOTOGRAFIE
\ STILLS

Haim Bargig

PROJEKTBETREUUNG
\ PROJECT MONITORING

Daniel Sponsel

HERSTELLUNGSLEITUNG
\ EXECUTIVE PRODUCTION

Mareike Lueg

HERSTELLUNGSASSISTENZ
\ PRODUCTION ASSISTANCE

Anna Katharina Engel

FILMGESCHÄFTSFÜHRUNG
\ PRODUCTION ACCOUNTANCE

Margit Werb

GESAMTLEITUNG
\ GENERAL DIRECTION

Prof. Heiner Stadler

ABBILDUNGSNACHWEIS
\ ILLUSTRATION CREDITS

25
© Bayerisches Landesamt für Denkmalpflege
Foto: Rupert Karbacher
27
© Bayerisches Nationalmuseum, München
33
© Bayerische Staatsbibliothek – Handschriftenabteilung
Foto: Silke Eberspächer
43
© Hochschule für Fernsehen und Film München
Fotos: Haim Bargig (4) und Steffen Weber (1)
16, 18, 20, 24, 26, 28, 30, 32, 34, 36, 38, 40
© Hochschule für Fernsehen und Film München
und Sanne Kurz, Udo Wrobel,
Katrin Jäger, Franziska von Malsen-Ponickau,
Lena Stahl, Johanna Thalmann und Steffen Weber
31
© Jüdisches Museum der Stadt Wien
19
© Jüdisches Museum München
17, 29, 35, 37, 39, 41
© Jüdisches Museum München
Fotos: Silke Eberspächer
21–23
© Metropolitankapitel Zu Unserer Lieben Frau, München
Foto: Silke Eberspächer